A Dales Walk

ALSO BY BOB ALLEN

On High Lakeland Fells

On Lower Lakeland Fells
also in paperback in separate volumes
Best Walks in the Lake District: The North-East, The South-East,
The North-West, The South-West

Escape to the Dales
also in paperback

On Foot in Snowdonia

Short Walks in the Lake District

with Peter Linney
Walking the Ridges of Lakeland
according to Wainwright's Pictorial Guides, Books 1–3

Walking More Ridges of Lakeland
according to Wainwright's Pictorial Guides, Books 4–7

A Dales Walk

Bob Allen

MICHAEL JOSEPH
LONDON

MICHAEL JOSEPH LTD

Published by the Penguin Group
27 Wrights Lane, London w8 5tz
Viking Penguin Inc., 375 Hudson Street, New York, New York 10014, USA
Penguin Books Australia Ltd, Ringwood, Victoria, Australia
Penguin Books Canada Ltd, 10 Alcorn Avenue, Toronto, Ontario, Canada m4v 3b2
Penguin Books (NZ) Ltd, 182–190 Wairau Road, Auckland 10, New Zealand

Penguin Books Ltd, Registered Offices: Harmondsworth, Middlesex, England

First published 1997
1 3 5 7 9 10 8 6 4 2

Copyright text and photographs © Bob Allen 1997
Copyright maps © Bob Allen and Michael Joseph Ltd 1997

Set in 11.5/15.5pt Monotype Bembo
Designed in QuarkXpress on an Apple Macintosh
Printed in Italy by L. E. G. O., Vicenza

A CIP catalogue record for this book is available from the British Library

ISBN 0 7181 4135 0
The moral right of the author has been asserted

Endpaper illustration: Field bottoms outside Thwaite, seen from the Pennine Way
Illustration on page i: Fields near Hardraw
on pages ii–iii: Mallerstang seen from the path to Swarth Fell

Contents

Introduction

For many walkers, including myself, the most satisfying walk is also a journey, starting in one place and finishing somewhere else some days later. Perhaps it is because the total experience is greater when you stay somewhere overnight and then carry on the following day; when you have made arrangements which oblige you to continue even in the face of a bad weather forecast. For there is great satisfaction in completing a journey once you have planned it, and a perverse pleasure to be gained from defying the elements. This Dales Walk is a journey of this type. As I walked the different high-level and low-level versions that are described here, my affection for these glorious dales has deepened enormously. I am quite sure that any walker will find the route as absorbing and the countryside as beautiful as I have done.

Unlike many of the long-distance walks that have been created over the last thirty years or so, this one is not a gruelling struggle. It was not my own idea, but that of my editor, Jenny Dereham, who asked me if I thought such a walk or journey as this was feasible and, if it were, would it be interesting. My initial reaction was that I thought it might be feasible and, if it were, then it would be enormously interesting. (Long after I had begun work myself, I discovered that there is a 55-mile circular walk, known as The Herriot Way and promoted by the Youth Hostels Association, which starts from Aysgarth Falls Youth Hostel and then, going anti-clockwise, links with the other Youth Hostels of Grinton, Keld and Hawes.) The walk described in this book covers some of the same ground but going clockwise, in the opposite direction, and the four Youth Hostels mentioned would certainly be excellent and appropriate stopping places, as will be evident from the text.

Of course, the original rough idea has been modified, improved and extended. The walk described in this book, that is the main walk, including its high-level variations, has been planned to be covered comfortably in one week of six days' walking, with a small amount of travel time by means other than your own legs being in addition. The main walk, if followed throughout, totals about 69 miles/110km; using all the high-level variations will give a walk of about 78 miles/125km. Strong walkers will no doubt be able to cover the ground in fewer than six days if they wish to do so.

Maps and Photographs

Most of the Walk can be followed using the OS 1:25 000 scale Outdoor Leisure 30 Yorkshire Dales Northern & Central areas. It omits Richmond, but only the final walk-in when it is impossible to go astray. And for that part of the Walk which goes into Mallerstang, Wild Boar Fell and the Kirkby Stephen area, walkers are now able to use the recently issued OS 1:25 000 scale Outdoor Leisure 19 Howgill Fells and Upper Eden Valley, which fulfils a long-standing need. These two maps are all that are necessary.

It is not easy to convey in a photograph the tranquil peace of a valley like Wensleydale when the sounds of running water, the wind in the trees and the songs of birds are obviously missing. I hope nevertheless that my photographs will do something to convey the special quality of these dales.

The Walk: A Synopsis

This book describes a walk which begins in Leyburn and then follows the course of the River Ure, on its south bank, from east to west up Wensleydale, to end the first day at Aysgarth, with its nationally famous waterfalls. This low-level stage is indeed all virtually on the level but it reveals a wealth of delightful unspoilt river scenery of far greater interest than can ever be depicted on a map (8 miles/12.8km). For walkers who are looking for more of a challenge, there is a high-level variation via the ancient town of Middleham, with its fine castle and echoes of Shakespeare's *Richard III*. This traverses the Middleham Gallops (where the racehorses are exercised) and then climbs to Penhill, the finest viewpoint in Wensleydale, before descending and traversing limestone edges to Aysgarth via the excavated ruins of a fourteenth-century Crusader Chapel (12½ miles/20km).

For the second day, the walk transfers to the north bank of the River Ure and traces a route at mid-level along a series of limestone terraces that give delightful walking, with traditional hay meadows and grassy pastures and with fine views across the middle and upper reaches of Wensleydale. Just before the end, it visits England's

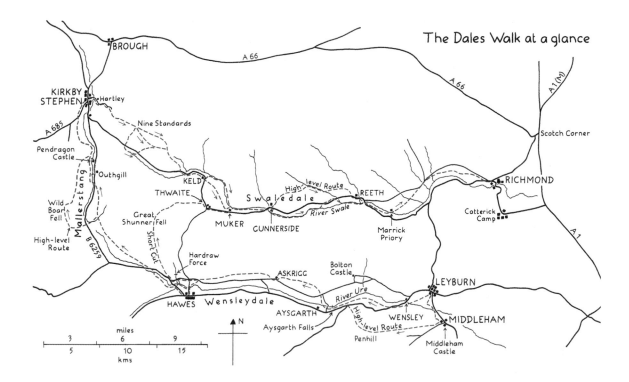

The Dales Walk at a glance

highest unbroken waterfall, Hardraw Force. There is accommodation either at Hardraw or, more probably, in the busy little nearby town of Hawes. A high-level variation is not legally feasible (12½ miles/20km).

The first two days' easy going should have got the walker into a higher gear for the third day. This is the longest, regardless of whether you take the high-level route or the main route at the lower level, but 15½ miles/24.8km for the main route and 19½ miles/31.2km for the full high-level way should not be excessive. Leaving Hawes (or Hardraw) the day's walking for both routes starts by climbing to the broad ridge of Cotter End, following the course of Lady Anne Clifford's Highway from west to north along a high-level limestone edge for several miles and then slanting down to the ravine of Hell Gill. At this point, 7½ miles/12km from the start, the walk splits into a low-level (main) and a high-level route. The low-level version continues as a gentle descent into the quiet Mallerstang valley and then shadows the course of the River Eden downstream to the romantic ruins of Pendragon Castle. The high-level variation leaves at Hell Gill Bridge, crosses the scenic Settle-to-Carlisle railway line at its highest point and then climbs to and traverses Wild Boar Fell before declining to the Mallerstang valley and joining the main route at Pendragon Castle. The conjoined routes continue to shadow the course of the River Eden, past the ruins of Lammerside Castle and into the town of Kirkby Stephen

The enigmatic stone cairns of the Nine Standards sit patiently on the skyline to the south-east of Kirkby Stephen and are the first objective for the fourth day, for which there is a single-level route – with seasonal variations. It is a steady climb from the valley of the River Eden back onto the high moorland overlooking the Stainmore Gap but then a gentle decline leads to the little village of Keld, at the head of the gorge of the River Swale, where the stage ends (10½ miles/16.8km).

As the late, great Alfred Wainwright wrote (in *A Coast to Coast Walk*): 'For most walkers the royal road from Keld to Reeth will always be along the lovely banks of the Swale, the first three miles to Muker especially being very beautiful.' Although AW's own walk then avoided those first three miles, the route taken for our fifth day makes full use of them, with a choice of paths down the sides of the Swale gorge itself. The first part, Keld to Gunnerside, is 5.3 miles/8.5km. Reaching Gunnerside, a walker wishing to leave the 'royal road' and see something of the remarkable remains of the lead-mining industry that dominated Swaledale until the end of the nineteenth century can follow a high-level version from Gunnerside to Reeth. (Totals for the day: Keld to Reeth via the main low-level route is 11¾ miles/18.8km; Keld to Reeth on the high-level version is 12¾ miles/20.4km.)

The sixth day follows the line taken by the 'Coast to Coast' path to the lovely town of Richmond, a splendid place at which to end a delightful journey (10½ miles/16.8km).

But that is not all. For any walker who feels that he or she must shorten the walk as a whole, there is a Short Cut over Great Shunner Fell, thus linking Wensleydale and Swaledale and omitting Mallerstang. (Hawes to Muker is about 10½ miles/16.8km.) That would reduce the six days to five, or less (as explained in more detail on page 118), depending how far you go beyond Muker down Swaledale that day. For walkers who may have more time at their disposal than a week, whose arrangements are flexible, or who return at a later date to explore further, the book ends with three circular walks. In addition, walkers could also make up their own two-day walks by using the main and alternative high-level routes in Days One, Three and Five.

Route Directions Only

Guidebooks are always a compromise. If this book had been offered as a pocket guide, in much smaller format, the illustrations also would have been much smaller, less interesting and much less appealing to those readers who are interested in the Dales because of their superb scenery and to whom high quality illustrations are important. However, with the needs of walkers in mind, the text of the route directions has been abbreviated and printed on pages at the back of the book, so that they may be easily consulted or perhaps even cut out carefully and taken on the walk itself. (If this sounds like a dreadful thing to do to a book, I have to confess to having done it myself for many years.)

Transport

Connections between Richmond and Leyburn for the first day are covered on page 1, although it must be mentioned here that bus services between Richmond and Leyburn on *Sundays* are non-existent. Apart from that, it is as well to note that bus services in the Dales tend to close down daily between approximately 0945 hrs and 1530 hrs. A complete list of bus and train times in the Yorkshire Dales National Park is given in the booklet *Dales Connections*, available free from the YDNP office at Grassington (*see* Addresses below) by sending a stamped addressed A5 envelope. Or copies can be picked up from either of the National Park Centres at Aysgarth Falls or Hawes. The Tourist Information Centres in Richmond and Leyburn (*see* Addresses below) are likely to have these, and any or all four centres are likely to be able to supply copies of the United Dalesbus Time Tables, as well as answer other enquiries concerning accommodation, taxi services etc. Some current taxi and bus operators' telephone numbers are supplied at the end of the list of Addresses (see below).

Accommodation

Youth Hostels
For those walkers who are members of the Youth Hostels Association (England and Wales) there should be no problems (in principle) at all, as there are Youth Hostels at the end of each of the stages suggested in this walk. (In Keld, the choice apart from the Youth Hostel is quite limited.) It may be worth pointing out to walkers who have perhaps not been YHA members for many years, if ever, that membership is not restricted in any way by your age, but by your own attitude. It only costs (in 1997) £9.50 per year for an adult to join, £3.50 for anyone under eighteen years of age; overnight stays are extremely reasonable and you can enjoy a good evening meal

and breakfast and even obtain a packed lunch for the following day. You will certainly meet other walkers and enjoy much friendship; it is well worth joining. When you do, you automatically receive the *YHA Accommodation Guide* which contains all that you need to know about Youth Hostels in Aysgarth, Hawes, Kirkby Stephen, Keld and Grinton (near Reeth), which are the stages used in this walk. This same handbook also contains many details about access by rail, bus and coach, with relevant telephone numbers.

Hotels, Inns, Bed-and-Breakfast Establishments

About two-thirds of this walk is within the boundary of the Yorkshire Dales National Park, the rest in Eden (East Cumbria). A good starting point for accommodation in the YDNP is the *Yorkshire Dales Accommodation Guide* published annually by the Yorkshire Dales National Park Committee (*see* Addresses below). For that part of the walk which is in the Mallerstang–Kirkby Stephen area (outside the YDNP boundary), the Kirkby Stephen Tourist Information Centre supply an *Accommodation Guide* (including where to eat) and local transport time-tables (*see* Addresses below). They may also be able to supply a copy of the *'Coast to Coast' Bed and Breakfast Accommodation Guide* which (for the purposes of this walk) is particularly good for all accommodation between Kirkby Stephen and Richmond. This will cost you £2.00 plus s.a.e. In the event of not being able to obtain this from Kirkby Stephen, you should contact Mrs Doreen Whitehead (*see* Addresses below) who, incidentally, has one of the few B&Bs in Keld.

In this booklet, an interesting service called 'The Coast to Coast Pack Horse' is advertised, which transports your backpack on a daily basis to various destinations, including Kirkby Stephen, Keld, Reeth and Richmond. Further information from Mr & Mrs Bowman, Kirkby Stephen (*see* Addresses below).

Camping and Camping Barns

There are formal camping sites at Aysgarth, Hawes, Keld and Richmond, but I have no doubt that a solo camper or a very small group of two or three walkers seeking to do this walk by camping overnight will be able to do so by asking permission first from farmers or landowners. I have met several walkers while en route myself who have done exactly that. Details of the formal camp sites will be found in the *Yorkshire Dales Accommodation Guide* mentioned above and obtainable from the YDNP offices. There is a camping barn at Leyburn at the start of the walk (details also in the *Accommodation Guide*) and bunkhouse and camping accommodation at Low Row in Swaledale as well as at East Applegarth Farm just outside Richmond (details in the Coast to Coast guide). The Youth Hostels Association, Northern

England office (*see* Addresses below) can also supply details of camping barns if you send them an s.a.e.

Refreshments

Refreshments for during the day do need to be considered the day before each stage. Most Youth Hostels, B&B establishments and inns offer packed lunches, but for other supplies only the larger places such as Leyburn, Middleham, Hawes, Kirkby Stephen and Richmond will be able to offer much choice. Smaller shops will be found in Aysgarth, Askrigg (where there is a good choice of eating-places), Muker, Gunnerside and Reeth, but post offices in many smaller places which might in the past have been relied upon for a packet of biscuits, a Mars Bar and a can of drink have either closed or are now only open on certain days: they should not be relied on. Where I spotted suitable places for refreshment, I have mentioned them in the specifications or the text. It is always advisable to carry your own water bottle or canned drinks.

Useful Names, Addresses, Telephone Numbers

1. Youth Hostels Association National Office, 8 St Stephen's Hill, St Albans, Hertfordshire AL1 2DY. Tel. 01727-85515, fax. 01727-844126.
2. Youth Hostels Association Northern England Office, PO Box 11, Matlock, Derbyshire DE4 2XA. Tel. 01629-825850, fax. 01629-824571.
3. Yorkshire Dales National Park, Hebden Road, Grassington, Skipton, North Yorkshire BD23 5LB. Tel. 01756-752748, fax. 01756-752745.
4. YDNP Centre, Aysgarth Falls. Tel. 01969-663424.
5. YDNP Centre, Station Yard, Hawes. Tel. 01969-667450.
6. Richmond Tourist Information Centre, Friary Gardens, Victoria Road, Richmond, North Yorkshire. Tel. 01748-850252.
7. Leyburn Tourist Information Centre, Thornborough Hall, Leyburn, North Yorkshire. Tel. 01969-622773.
8. Kirkby Stephen Tourist Information Centre, Market Square, Kirkby Stephen, Cumbria CA17 4QN. Tel. 017683-71199.
9. Mrs Doreen Whitehead, East Stonesdale Farm, Keld, North Yorkshire DL11 6LJ. Tel. 01748-886374 (for *Coast to Coast Accommodation Guide* etc).
10. Mr & Mrs Bowman, West View Farmhouse, Hartley, Kirkby Stephen, Cumbria CA17 4JH. Tel/fax. 017683-71680 (for 'Coast to Coast Pack Horse').

11. United Dalesbus: Tel. 01325-468771 (for up to date bus times in Wensleydale and Swaledale).

12. Some taxi operators in Richmond:
    D & J Taxis   01748-825112
    HK Taxis   01748-822323
    Trinity Cabs   01748-822269

13. Some taxi operators in Leyburn:
    BMW Taxis   01969-622604
    Elk Taxis   01969-622882
    G. A. Private Hire   01969-622790

14 A taxi operator in Hawes:
    Town Head Garage   01969-667483

15. Some taxi operators in Kirkby Stephen:
    J D Taxis   017683-71682
    John Thompson   017683-71741

Acknowledgements

In addition to my editor, Jenny Dereham, without whose idea the book would not have been created and whose editing skills have, as always, polished and improved my work enormously, I must gratefully acknowledge the help I have received from Mr Dick Capel of the East Cumbria Countryside Project in connection with some parts of the route in Mallerstang and elsewhere, and Mr H.T. Thornton-Berry of Swinithwaite, Leyburn, in respect of part of the high-level alternative route where it touches Penhill. My debt to the Ordnance Survey will be obvious.

I should also mention here that this book has been compiled in accordance with the 'Guidelines for the Writers of Path Guides' produced by the Outdoor Writers' Guild. These are too long to reproduce here, but walkers may take comfort from the knowledge that all reasonable care has been taken to see that they will not be heading into confrontations with landowners as a result of following directions in this book.

The Walk: Getting Started

The walk begins in Leyburn and is described in a clockwise direction, going from south to north so that it ends at Richmond. I wish it would have been possible to make it a complete circuit on foot, but MoD training grounds between Leyburn and Richmond make this impractical, unless you want to walk the connecting 12 miles/19.2km along the main road. I certainly would not do that myself and I cannot see anyone else finding it much fun either. The shape of the walk is, therefore, that of an elongated horseshoe and I strongly recommend that the two ends be linked using wheels rather than feet.

I hope that this walk will be attractive to people of all ages, some of whom will own cars, some of whom will be relying on public transport; some will be tied to a fixed length of holiday and some will have no fixed time-table: such variations make it difficult to be specific about how best to link Richmond and Leyburn, but the following notes will, I hope, be useful.

By car: Leyburn and Richmond are both easily reached from the A1.
By rail or coach: the nearest big town is Darlington and there are connections by bus from there, also some from Northallerton (United Dalesbus time-table enquiries 01325-468771).

Both Leyburn and Richmond have lots of B&B and hotel accommodation and both are busy places, with shopping and eating facilities open every day of the week including Sundays. Walkers with their own transport may choose to leave it either in Richmond or Leyburn; those coming by public transport may arrive at either place, so the links between the two towns needs to be mentioned.

The 12 miles or so between them takes about half an hour by bus. The bus service times given below were correct at time of writing but may of course change. There are other services in addition. For enquiries telephone 01325-468771.

The main service is United's no. 26, which leaves Richmond Market Place at 0830 on Saturday, at 0925 on Tuesday, Friday and Saturday and at 0950 on Monday, Wednesday and Thursday; there is no Sunday service. If you miss it, there is a service in the afternoons at around 1500hrs (the times vary by a few minutes each day).

If these times prove inconvenient, there may be a great deal to be said for simply taking a taxi: I was quoted a price (1996) of £8–£10 between Richmond and Leyburn which I thought was reasonable. Taxis are normally to be found in Richmond's Market Place at all times of the day and evening; *see also* the telephone numbers supplied on page xiv.

Bearing in mind that the main walk (low-level, Leyburn to Aysgarth) on the first day is only a distance of 8 miles/12.8km, it is quite feasible, with pre-booked accommodation for the first night at least, to complete it having started in the afternoon. Walkers planning to use the Youth Hostels are strongly advised to pre-book, especially during the summer months.

Just one last insidious thought: any walker arriving in Leyburn (or leaving Leyburn having stayed there overnight) to do the high-level variation on the first day and feeling a little pressed for time, might judge that the first hour that would be spent walking between Leyburn and Middleham could be more profitably employed visiting Middleham Castle. There are only two buses a week to Middleham, so it is not worth bothering with them. On the other hand, a taxi will only cost about £3.

A typical Dales meadow, near Sedbusk

Day One

Leyburn to Aysgarth

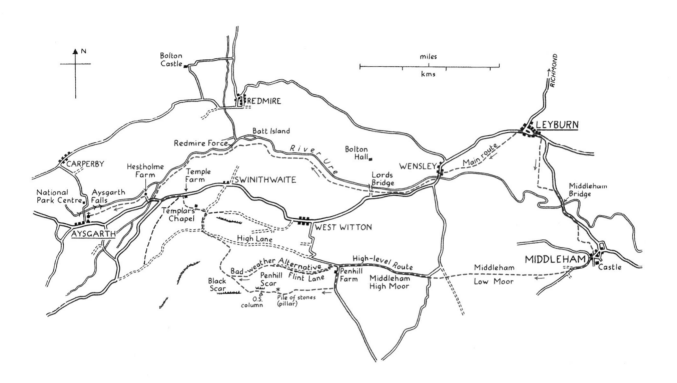

Perhaps rather confusingly, a walk up Wensleydale does not trace the course of the River Wensley (which does not exist) but follows the course of the River Ure (or, in earlier times, 'Yore'). In years immediately after the Norman Conquest, the valley was indeed known as 'Yoredale', a name which survives in geology to identify the Yoredale Series of rocks found in the area and which were quarried to provide 'Yoredale flags'. These did not flap from flag poles but roofed (and still do roof) traditional Dales houses, and the workings from which they were won are still plainly visible: many disused ones will be seen along the way, but there must be others still in production in less obvious places.

Wensleydale takes its name from the little village of Wensley at the eastern end of the valley where the now fat and lazy Ure meanders between two final areas of slightly higher land before drifting gently into the plains beyond. On the northern slope is the busy little town of Leyburn, where the walk begins. On the southern of those two areas lie the towers and battlements of Middleham Castle: the high-level variation of the walk goes from Leyburn via Middleham (*see* page 17).

At the centre of Leyburn, the main commercial centre of Wensleydale, lies its bustling Market Place, a large rectangular open space, on a slight slope, with fine mellow buildings, shops, cafés, B&Bs and hotels lining its perimeter. One of those hotels, the Bolton Arms, stands imposingly in the corner at the upper (north-western) end of the Place, and from here departs the A684 road heading for Wensley, the Aysgarth Falls and, in due course, Hawes. It is our starting point for a day of peaceful pastures, river, woods and waterfalls.

Main (low-level) Route

- ➤ *Distance:* **About 8 miles/12.8km**
- ➤ *Altitude gained:* **Negligible**
- ➤ *Terrain:* **On generally good paths, mostly over well-drained limestone pastures giving easy and very pleasant walking.**
- ➤ *Refreshments:* **Leyburn is the place to stock up before starting the walk; the only other possibility may be in Wensley, but it is only half an hour's walking from Leyburn.**

Leyburn to Wensley

Leaving the Market Place, walk down a tarmac footpath alongside the main carriageway towards Hawes and in about 150 yds or so, on the left and opposite the driveway into a bungalow, watch for a 'public footpath' finger-post pointing half-left (southwest) across a field.

Immediately, if you have not already noticed it before now, your eye will be drawn to the bulk of Penhill, a round hump of high land on the skyline on the other side of the broad valley spread before you and the highest land in sight. The way ahead to Wensley is essentially towards Penhill and it is useful to bear this in mind, for this path does not seem much used at the time of writing.

Fortunately, although the land is parcelled up into numerous fields by stone walls, stiles of one kind or another – be they slit-stiles, step-stiles or occasional ladder-stiles

Penhill seen from just outside Leyburn ➤

– can almost always be spotted ahead to ensure that the path is not lost. Yellow arrow way-marks nailed to handy posts and trees are also a useful confirmation. Once Wensley Bridge has been reached, the paths on the next stretch, beside the River Ure, are more trodden and obvious. Although some of these first fields are ploughed for cultivation, my observation is that this will be found to be unusual on this walk; almost all the cultivated land that is crossed is used only for grazing.

   At the far side of the first field the way leads via two ladder-stiles across the Wensleydale railway line. This used to carry stone from the quarry above Redmire but fell into dis-use after the quarry was closed. It has, however, been re-opened as, I understand, an ecological means of transporting military tanks from the Catterick complex to Salisbury Plain. Another nearby ladder-stile and a slit-stile immediately after it lead to the corner of a large field, which is ploughed from time to time, but turn right along its top edge, with a hedge on the right, then stiles lead just to the left of a dilapidated barn and outbuildings and then to a gate, where, on the right, can be seen the goalposts of Wensleydale RUFC. As soon as you have crossed a stile at the side of an old bath used as a cattle-trough, you turn sharp left and pass down the field beyond for 100 yds and then back sharp right at another stile, thus regaining the original south-westerly direction. After one more slit-stile the path trends more

noticeably downhill towards a small plantation, crossing the wall on its right just before reaching it and then going left, just above the plantation, to follow the left edge of the field beyond round to the right.

The way now runs parallel to the River Ure, seen below for the first time, and the houses of Wensley village appear ahead. A stile on the approach to a square-built detached house is the last, for beyond it you cross the paddock left of the building (the left fork shown on the OS map) to a gate leading onto a metalled lane. Turn left here, downhill, and this lane swings left between a few houses to reach a minor road. As soon as you have turned right here, the fine medieval parish church of the Holy Trinity will be seen facing you across the road.

This is well worth a visit, particularly if you have the whole afternoon ahead to complete the stage to Aysgarth. Apparently parts of the structure of the church date back to 1245 – a date so far back in time that it is difficult to begin to imagine the lives of the local population here then – although the square tower was built in the early seventeenth century. I had heard that its interior was of great interest and I was glad of the opportunity to visit it. A notice beside the door of the church giving instructions for brass rubbing immediately set me looking for whatever it is that brass rubbers rub. It did not take me long to find at least one item, for on the floor of the sanctuary I found a splendid and highly-polished brass memorial to one of the rectors of the parish, in the shape of a figure looking like a crusader in armour, with arms crossed over his chest. The choir stalls and pulpit have some fine carved wood gleaming with the polish of ages but the box pew built exclusively for the Scropes, later the Bolton family dominates the interior, as the family dominated much of surrounding Wensleydale. The screenwork around the pew is intricately carved and came (I suppose the modern words would be 'was lifted') from Easby Abbey at the Dissolution.

I wandered around, hoping for some gleams of light by which to take photographs and as I did so a gentleman in a dog collar marched in briskly and took some snap shots with a flash gun. He was the vicar of Middleham and told me that he was doing a survey of church buildings in the area, to establish which, if any, could be used for purposes other than those for which they were originally intended. As he pointed out, there was not much hope of Wensley Church being used for anything other than worship. Although, like the majority of my friends and neighbours nowadays, I am only an occasional churchgoer – weddings, funerals and the great festivals of Christmas and Easter comprise my own attendance as a rule – I could not help but feel vaguely upset and disquieted by the implications of his remarks. There are some parts of our cultural heritage that just have to be preserved and preferably still functioning; surely wonderful buildings like this, which encapsulate bits of the history of

Bolton Hall seen from Lords Bridge ➤

our remarkable nation and put us in touch with aspects of its life that are rapidly being lost, is one of them.

Leaving the church and turning left, across the main road (A684) is the drive that leads to Bolton Hall, family seat of the largest landowners in the area; I could just imagine the horse-drawn carriages cantering along it and their occupants then walking proudly to their private pews for morning service. The little village of Wensley itself, however, lost its own high status as being the only market town in the valley when its inhabitants were almost completely annihilated by plague in 1563. The village never recovered from the blow and nearby Leyburn took over the market activity.

Incidentally, the monks of Jervaulx Abbey, just a few miles further down the valley and who probably owned much of the land around Wensley at the time, are believed to have been the inventors of Wensleydale Cheese, originally made from ewe's milk, although cow's milk was soon used thereafter.

Wensley to Lords Bridge

Turn left onto the main A684, and continue on the main road for 150 yds to cross the River Ure by Wensley Bridge. Immediately after the last stone support has been passed, look for a footpath on the right.

This path, although initially quite narrow, is evidently well used. It picks its way through tall grasses, saplings and woodland, at times along the top of a sort of embankment, and there are plenty of roots and other obstacles to contend with. The sudden alarmed squawk of pheasants in the undergrowth occasionally startles as you proceed, shadowing the river which, when you can see it, is here about 10 yds wide. Occasionally you hear the gurgle and splash of water over stony shallows, but more often the river runs deep and quietly, patrolled by moorhens and mallard

After about ¾ mile, the path passes through a cleared area, close to the main road which is on the left. It then traverses a small plantation of young oak saplings whose immature trunks are protected by plastic tubes; it seems very clear that within a few years these trees will be blocking the way and the path will have to be re-routed slightly. Beyond the path rises slightly to a gate and then shadows the river at a higher level to reach a slit-stile giving access to the private drive (but public footpath) leading to Bolton Hall on the far (north) side of the river. The drive crosses the Ure to approach the hall by Lords Bridge and it is worth strolling the 50 yds or so down the drive to the bridge for a good view of the countryside upstream, but also for a view of Bolton Hall itself.

Bolton Hall is a large and well-proportioned building, seen beyond two pillars with stone balls on top that stand sentinel at the bridge. There is a lot of old ivy on its walls, a splendid weather-vane on its roof and many Georgian-style windows on its south-facing front, which overlooks lawns and almost flat meadowland sweeping down to the banks of the river. It was apparently built by the Duke of Bolton in 1678 after he married the daughter of the last Lord Scrope and came into possession of the Scrope lands. These must have been substantial, for the Scropes of Danby were one of the most powerful families in the north of England in their time. A flash of memory from my distant days as a student of history reminds me that a Scrope was Chancellor to King Richard II (the one before Shakespeare's crook-backed Richard of Gloucester who became Richard III). But the night Bolton Hall was extensively damaged by fire in 1902 must have been one of the biggest bonfires Wensleydale has ever seen. It has, of course, been rebuilt since then and, I believe, still contains many fine paintings. Just to see this fine house from Lords Bridge is to get a whiff of an era when ownership of land was the only kind that counted. Such innovations as Planning Authorities, who can tie private owners into knots but seem not to be able to prevent many farmers allowing their premises to look like agricultural slums, had not been invented.

The River Ure: looking towards Redmire from Lords Bridge ➤

Lords Bridge to Redmire Force

Retracing the few steps back up the drive to where the footpath crosses it by slit-stiles, a delightful grass path over underlying limestone continues upstream, shadowing the river, which is now temporarily out of sight. Two more slit-stiles show the way ahead but the path is over firm limestone pastures which tend not to retain the imprint of footprints so it is not very clear across a long field until a gate is reached at the edge of a small stream. A finger-post just beyond the footbridge by which the beck is crossed gives two forward directions: one for 'High Wanless', the other for 'Hestholme Br for West Burton & Aysgarth'. It is the latter, the one trending right (north-west) which you need and a step-stile leads over the nearby fence and you are soon back on the river bank again. More delightful and easy walking follows through a pleasant parkland of pastures dotted with ash, sycamore and especially fine beech trees which line the bank on this south side and also border West Wood on the other bank, opposite. Their smooth grey trunks are unmistakable, and the many rabbits diving into burrows under their huge roots are

even more numerous than the pheasants that strut cockily along ahead of you. They only take to flight when danger seems especially close. It was as well that I did not have my dogs with me or they would have been sorely tempted to grab at departing tail feathers.

At the west end of the wooded Batt Island, which divides the river temporarily, pale grey limestone clints stick up out of the river bed at times of low water, making soothing gurgles, but in a further ¼ mile the path climbs onto some higher land on the south bank and you can see and hear how the river rushes noisily over stony shallows and into a narrow where this higher ground forces the river round a bend until it empties into a wide pool.

The way continues upstream close to the river for a short way, but then cuts across a particularly wide bend. You are now almost opposite Redmire, one of the larger settlements in Wensleydale, but you can see nothing of it as you are screened by trees from all but the close surroundings. The land here would be level as a cricket pitch if it were not for a great number of small grass and moss-topped hummocks which all seem to have rabbit holes beside them. This must be Rabbit City although, strangely, I did not see a single one. Just beyond, still keeping close to a wall bounding the woodland on the right, the way climbs slightly to cross a zone of much larger and distinctive grassy limestone hummocks. A tractor track leads from here towards the farm buildings at Swinithwaite, which can just be distinguished up the slopes on the left, with the scarps of several limestone shelves rising beyond them to the heights of Penhill. The line of the path runs briefly beside this track but then reaches a ladder-stile over a wall. Here a notice erected by the Countryside Commission concerning the Countryside Stewardship Scheme displays a map showing two areas of private land where 'you are free to wander'. This scheme (now taken over by the Min. of Ag.) seems to be receiving growing support from landowners and must be welcomed by all responsible walkers.

At the far right-hand side, which is also the top edge, of this hummocky pasture is a gate and finger-post into some woodland, and the sound of the river is suddenly very loud and near. In a further 50 yds you find yourself on the river bank again, but now high above it, with the cataracts of Redmire Force pouring over three separate limestone sills below. While there are bigger waterfalls to come ahead, these are still impressive; even better, you will be almost certain to be able to enjoy them on your own, for it takes too much effort for the motorized tourist to get here from Aysgarth. I found this a grand place to sit for a while and have a bite to eat. I then followed the path as it descended to the water's edge for the best view of the upper section of the falls.

Redmire Force to Aysgarth

From this point I was somewhat surprised to find a made path – a ramp and some steps – leading up the bank to a wicket-gate. I expected to see a well-used path now heading for Aysgarth but instead found the way hardly discernible on the ground. It is, however, clearly indicated by the line of slit-stiles heading across more pastures and alongside the edge of a wood shielding the river from view again as it flows through a tree-filled ravine below. Emerging from the shelter of the wood you suddenly obtain a fine view of Bolton Castle, its mellow stone glowing in sunlight, on the other side of the river. This will come into view on several more occasions and it is such a dominating feature of the landscape that, although it is impractical to visit on this walk, a little more about it may well be of interest.

Bolton Castle certainly still looks as if it would have been capable of repelling all but the most determined enemy, with its tall square towers, battlements and arrow slits, but when put to the test during the Civil War – when it harboured a royalist garrison – it surrendered in 1645 after being besieged by the Roundheads. It was evidently built, initially as a fortified manor house, by the first Lord Scrope, and the

Bolton Castle, evening

work of construction, which began in 1379, took eighteen years. (Imagine going to your bank or building society and telling them that construction was going to take eighteen years and could you please have a bridging loan ...) Bolton Castle, however, is surely best known for its romantic connection with Mary Queen of Scots who, after her flight from Scotland to Carlisle, was imprisoned here for seven months from July 1568 to January 1569, in the care of the ninth Lord Scrope, then Governor of Carlisle. It was an 'imprisonment' which seems to have been endured in some comfort since she evidently arrived with six personal attendants and forty others, which must have put quite a strain on the Scropes. It was from here that Mary made her famous attempt to escape, but only got as far as the the outskirts of Leyburn. Queen Elizabeth I and her advisers had problems in knowing quite how to deal with this dangerous prisoner and shifted uneasily from steel fist to velvet glove in their treatment of her. It does seem, however, that her attempt at escape showed the Scropes to be careless gaolers, so Mary was removed from Bolton Castle, beginning a journey that only ended for her on the scaffold.

More trees shortly close off the view across the river and finger-posts lead you down towards the corner of a wood, ahead. This is Wellclose Plantation and a ladder-stile slightly up a slope on the left, as well as a gate lower down and to the right of the ladder-stile, suggests that the way must be in this direction. Not so: the ladder-stile leads into an enclosed coppice used for feeding and rearing pheasants and the gate simply leads to another gate and then into an enclosed field with no obvious escape. The key to this tricky bit, the only place on this stretch from Wensley Bridge where the way was not evident to me within seconds, is to veer to the right and down the slope to keep close to the wall shadowing the river. Then a finger-post and step-stile will be spotted beneath some beech trees, with the footpath showing clearly, descending a short but fairly steep bank beneath the trees to rejoin the river bank.

Here you almost immediately come across a notice rather intriguingly reading 'Dangerous ford ahead at present impassable'. It is as well that you do not wish to cross for there looks to be little sign of anything resembling a ford. The message is evidently intended for someone travelling in the opposite direction (west to east) and you are now at Slapestone Wath where Stony Stoop Lane used to cross the river by the ford and join Thoresby Lane to connect with the village of Castle Bolton beyond (the castle is Bolton Castle, the village is Castle Bolton). Incidentally, Stony Stoop Lane is shown as a walled lane on the OS 1:25 000 maps but there is almost no sign now of one of the walls and only a trace on the ground of the course of the lane. The stones have no doubt been utilised elsewhere.

Crossing two more fields, the way now leads obviously towards a ladder-stile over a wall and then veers right towards a building at Adam Bottoms. This was clearly

The River Ure, immediately downstream of Aysgarth Lower Force ➤

once a farmhouse which, when I was last there, was being renovated. Pass in front of the house to a seven-barred iron gate found up a little slope just beyond and then, shadowing the Walden Beck which joins the Ure at the delightfully named Froddle Dub, two more slit-stiles enable you to step onto the tarmac of the A684. Turn right to cross the Walden Beck by Hestholme Bridge.

There is a finger-post on the right at the entrance to the drive to Hestholme Farm immediately beyond the bridge and this points you on a well-used path across a level pasture towards the bank of the River Ure once more and it can now be heard again if not yet seen. Two wicket-gates lead quickly to the margin, close by a series of small cascades, then the path starts to climb a slope and it becomes clear that the river, which is quite wide here and flowing over limestone pavement below, is emerging from a vertically-sided rocky gorge. Although the OS map shows the path splitting, with one branch going along the bank, it is in fact channelled by a fence so it climbs up the slope above and to the left of the gorge, probably to avoid the risk of accidents. Aysgarth Lower Force, where the waters pour over four distinct rock lips, can be seen below, though not very well from this bank.

Rather annoyingly, the path now rises higher but also further away from the river, which is screened by trees, so that you only get a glimpse of the majestic Middle Force. It is time to make a definite resolution to get to the other bank for a proper view: it is well worth it and can be done shortly. In the meantime, the footpath leads

through a small sycamore plantation, emerging on the edge of a field with the fine sight of St Andrew's Church, Aysgarth, directly opposite.

The church has a fine tower with six spiky pinnacles adorning its top. It also has a clock that tells the correct time (quite rare) and a fine set of Westminster chimes. As the footpath leads through the graveyard surrounding it, containing many tilted gravestones, you also pass its front door. You should therefore have no difficulty in taking a respectful look inside your second ancient Dales church of the day and, like Wensley's church, it is well worth it to see the fine stained-glass windows and especially the famous rood screen. A notice inside tells that this, and the vicar's stall, was the work of the School of Ripon carvers of about 1506 and was taken from Jervaulx Abbey in 1536 when it was dissolved on the orders of Henry VIII. It can be illuminated by a fluorescent light, which shows its structure and the red, gold and blue colours in which it is painted to good effect, although the blue looks rather green under the artificial light.

Aysgarth, and the Aysgarth Falls in particular, is one of the 'honeypot' areas of the Yorkshire Dales and there is therefore a lot to be said for leaving your visit to the

The Jervaulx rood screen in St Andrew's, Aysgarth

Falls until later in the day, when many visitors will have departed. In any event, you will probably feel inclined to ensure that your own first night's lodging is secure so, on leaving the church, turn right outside its front door and the path leads directly to the road, on a fairly steep hill. A right turn here, downhill, would lead to the River Ure and the various waterfalls but a left turn, uphill, shortly passes a convenient café on the left. The Youth Hostel is immediately beyond it on the junction with the A684 and to the left, with a hotel (The Palmer Flatts Hotel) on the junction to the right. For other accommodation for this first night, either continue to the junction and turn right along the main road into the village of Aysgarth, or take a path from just opposite the church, signed to the village.

If you are staying at the Youth Hostel and arrange to purchase a packed lunch for tomorrow, there will be no problem with supplies; otherwise there is a good shop in the village. Askrigg, reached at about lunchtime tomorrow, has a good choice of eating places.

Nobody should visit Aysgarth and fail to visit the falls, cascades or waterfalls of the River Ure, which are named as High Force, Middle Force and Lower Force by the OS, so those are the names used in this book although the YDNP signs all use 'Falls'. As mentioned above, if, instead of turning uphill on leaving St Andrew's, you turn right and go downhill round a bend to the river, you will see the Aysgarth High Force sideways on. Overhung by fine trees across much of their width, these are pretty as the waters splash over a series of limestone sills, and are particularly impressive at times of flood.

Immediately beyond these, the road crosses the river by the narrow Yore Bridge but, before crossing, you will also see a sign, on the building itself, advertising the G. W. Shaw Carriage Museum of Horse-drawn Vehicles. This is open to the public seven days a week, 9.30 a.m. until dusk except during the winter months, and is well worth a visit. The steps on leaving provide an excellent place from which to take photographs of the falls incidentally. The building was a water-powered cotton mill during the eighteenth century, which was fairly unusual as cotton mills were much more associated with Lancashire. In the mid nineteenth century, it was re-built and became a wool-spinning mill; then it turned to milling flour, an activity lasting until 1968.

Having crossed Yore Bridge, turn left through a kissing-gate and follow a tarmac footpath signed 'National Park Centre' which leads to the complex of car park, café, toilets, giftshop and information source. From here, more signs point the way to the broad path leading towards the various viewing places for the Middle Force and the Lower Force. Alternatively, having crossed Yore Bridge, follow the road, rather than the tarmac path, up the slope to the right to find the same broad path signposted on

Aysgarth Middle Force in flood

the right-hand side of the road. The Middle Force is the one normally reached first and the waters, falling over two tiers, are usually quite turbulent. The path continues to a point where you can easily descend to the limestone floor at the foot of the gorge for a close view of the Lower Force

High-level variation via Penhill

➤ *Distance:* About 12½ miles/20km
➤ *Altitude gained:* About 1400 ft/427m
➤ *Terrain:* Mostly on well-drained grassy limestone shelves with a short section of road walking, and some peatier ground on the gritstone moorland of Penhill.
➤ *Refreshments:* Pub, tea shops, etc., in Middleham, but this is only a short way from Leyburn. No other facilities until Aysgarth Falls.

The high-level alternative to the first day of this walk takes you to Penhill, surely the finest viewpoint in Wensleydale. From Leyburn the route follows field paths towards a crossing of the River Ure at Middleham Bridge. Then a little road walking and more field paths complete the stage to Middleham. The route then traverses Middleham Low, then the High Moor to Penhill Farm, beyond which it climbs to Penhill. It contours westwards above Penhill Scar then descends to the old Penhill Quarry to join High Lane and visit the Templars Chapel before the final stretch into Aysgarth.

Leyburn to Middleham

When in Leyburn's Market Place turn south-east, on the A684 towards Bedale and Northallerton (heading away from the Bolton Arms) and towards the tall square tower of St Matthew's church. This is visible from the market place and is located just beyond the point where it narrows to the width of the main road. Directly opposite is a 'public footpath' finger-post pointing south. The metalled path almost immediately crosses the railway line by a stone bridge, turning right, then left down steps on its far side (yellow arrows) to pass the entrance to a bungalow, then continues as a good track between houses as far as a metalled road serving a small estate of houses. Turn right, then immediately left here through a stone slit-stile and, going south, follow a grassy trod (yellow arrows) down two fields of sheep pasture via gateways into a narrow field which has some trees (and a little stream to ford on big stones) at its far end. The stile here is directly next to the stream. Crossing this, keep close to the fence on the right and, continuing south, reach one more stile in the right-hand corner of the field before a short descent leads to a junction with a minor road (Low Lane). (The OS map shows an apparent short-cut path, going left to the bottom of Mighten's Bank, but it is not easily spotted, has some awkward and not easily seen stiles and is best avoided.)

Turn left along Low Lane, which has a wide grass verge, and shortly turn right on reaching the A6108. Middleham Bridge, across the River Ure, can be seen ¼ mile ahead, with the towers and ramparts of Middleham Castle on the near skyline. The long green whaleback of land stretching westwards in the middle distance, forming a subsidiary ridge between Coverdale and Wensleydale, is Middleham Low Moor and our walk traverses it.

Reaching Middleham Bridge, you cannot fail to notice that it has four stone towers, one at each corner, with what look like arrow slits and you would not be overly surprised if a drawbridge clanged down and men armed with pikes and staves surrounded you as you attempted to cross it. It is only wide enough for a single vehicle, so cross with care. On the far side walk along the road for a further ¼ mile until you reach some bungalows on the right. Just past the second bungalow you will find a public footpath sign where a short ladder-stile leads over a wall on the right and across the edge of a garden to a gate into a sloping field. Turn left (more arrows) along the edge of the field, at the back of some more bungalows, and then up the pastures beyond, via two stiles, towards more houses ahead. Fifty yards before reaching them, the path is signed to the left (east), alongside a very substantial wall, to reach a tarmac road at the edge of a small housing estate.

Turn half-right here and yellow arrows mark a good footpath behind some houses and, via two slit-stiles, across a meadow, to enter the grounds of Middleham's square-towered parish church, seen directly ahead. Just before reaching the church, turn half-right at the tall cross of the war memorial. (The word 'Death' on it faces you as you approach, but do not let that put you off: it is because 'Faithful unto Death' is carved on different facets and you are only seeing one of them on this approach.) A narrow, paved passage now leads between a high wall and some houses; when it ends, turn half-left at a minor road and the grey stones of Middleham Castle will be seen directly ahead across an open space furnished with a memorial to Queen Victoria. Turning left, downhill, will take you to the adjacent market square, the other open space in the middle of the town, where there is an ancient cross as well as pubs, cafés and other useful facilities.

Middleham Castle is run by English Heritage and is open 10 a.m. to 4 p.m. daily during the summer season (with a long list of different times at other seasons) but it is well worth visiting. It was begun, like other Norman castles, about 1170, in the century after the Conquest and intended as a stronghold from which the newly conquered lands could be firmly controlled. Two centuries later it had passed into the

Looking west from the ramparts of Middleham Castle ➤

hands of the powerful Neville family, whose head was then Richard Neville, Earl of Warwick, known to history and William Shakespeare as the 'Kingmaker'. On Warwick's death the castle passed to the crown and Edward IV gave it to his brother, the infamous 'Crookback' who is believed to have had the 'Princes in the Tower' murdered because they were obstacles in his way to assuming the crown himself, as Richard III. Shakespeare's version of this story has passed into legend, although modern studies apparently show Richard in a much more favourable light and not the black villain that we have all loved to hate. He held his court here: for a while the centre of political power in England was in Yorkshire (and no less than was right and proper, say thousands of stout Yorkshiremen!).

The castle was not involved in the Civil War, but the Parliamentarians ordered its destruction in 1646, in common with all similar strongholds. Fortunately for us, the work of demolition was only partly done and the walls of the massive keep are even now almost their original height. These, with the deep moat, the banqueting hall, the chapel and gatehouse all show what a remarkable fortress stood, and still stands here.

Middleham's castle and history (not to mention the 'Middleham jewel' found in a nearby field only a few years ago) is fascinating, but what is perhaps even more

interesting is the fact that this tiny town has (or at least has recently had) as many as twenty-two different stables for racehorses. If you are in Middleham in the afternoon you will not necessarily see any sign of a horse, but a discreet peep, for instance, down the ginnels behind the castle will soon disclose rows of loose-boxes with horses' heads sticking out of them. In the mornings, however, you are left in no doubt at all that racehorses are the business here and have evidently been so since the monks of nearby Jervaulx and Coverham Abbeys bred them and trained them on the splendid expanses of Middleham Low Moor which our walk shortly also crosses.

Middleham to Penhill Farm

Leave Middleham by the Coverdale road, the one leading uphill to the south-west next to the castle ruins. It is fairly narrow and walled initially on both sides, but in about 300 yds the high wall on the right turns sharply away and that on the left bends away, so that you emerge onto a wide, open and grassy moor. Directly ahead a sign reading 'Racehorses' will confirm that you are now on Middleham Low Moor and all that has to be done is to walk its length westwards. The unmistakable humped shape of Penhill is due west; it can be seen for almost all the way and is therefore an infallible guide to your direction.

As you look for a footpath to get you started, you will no doubt see, on the sharp-

Racehorses returning to Middleham from the gallops

angled corner of the moor close by, a 'public bridleway' sign, pointing just a few degrees south of west. There is, however, no indication on the ground of any trod of use to a foot passenger; up here horses reign. The gravel track over on the right beside a wall, also heading west, looks promising but is, as you may well find out if you are here in the morning when the racehorses are being exercised, used both by horses and by their trainers in cars, so it is as well avoided. The best thing to do is to walk along the Coverdale road for a further 70 yds or so to where there is a pull-in for vehicles, and step off the tarmac there. Directly ahead you will then see a narrow strip of different coloured earth rising straight up the gentle slope ahead; on closer acquaintance, this will be seen to be a man-made gallops of raked sand and grit about 8 ft wide. Believe me, when the horses come pounding up that, they are going like the clappers and you do not want to be in their way. The gallops are in fact north of the green-pecked public bridleway which is shown on the OS map but is not evident on the ground, so by keeping left of the gallops you are almost certainly on the line of the public bridleway, walking over springy grass towards Penhill.

The end of the gallops is marked by white-painted fencing and the horses come pounding up the incline and then swing to the right to go back, so keep 30 yds or so left of it for safety. Shortly after the gallops end, spot a standing stone about 5ft high about 100 yds away on the right, and 150 yds further on there is a trig point, on the highest bit of this very flattened bit (Cross Bank). There is a good view from here across Wensleydale to Leyburn.

The trig point is on Cross Bank and from there onwards the way – it can only be 'way' for there is no definite path – undulates westwards over a couple of low grassy humps, always heading for Penhill. It then crosses a gravel track to emerge at a junction of three roads. The one directly ahead is Common Lane, and you take it across Middleham High Moor to Penhill Farm.

The lane is walled for almost half a mile but is unfrequented and almost level until, after a little dip, it rises slightly. Now the wall on the left becomes a fence and that on the right falls back to leave a wide strip of grass that gives pleasanter walking. Common Lane runs along the top of a limestone shelf at the top of Capple Bank, with a larch plantation below, and from the edge of the escarpment there are extensive views across Wensleydale, to Bolton Hall and also, if you look carefully, ahead and to the right, to Bolton Castle. Middleham High Moor, to the left of the road, is clearly also laid out for training racehorses but at the time of writing is closed for that purpose.

At the end of Common Lane, the road veers right down the fierce bends of Witton Steeps to West Witton, but turn left on to the road signed for Melmerby and Carlton to pass the buildings of Penhill Farm on the right.

Penhill Farm to High Lane via Penhill Scar

➤   (For a bad-weather alternative route, *see* page 26)

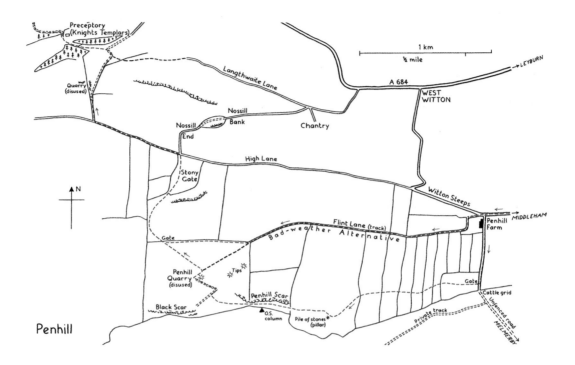

From Penhill Farm, the road climbs gently until, just before the crest of the hill ahead and 50 yds before reaching some white-painted gates across the road on either side of a cattle-grid, there is a gate into a field on the right, and a sign reading 'BW Penhill'. Leaving the road here, a grassy trod now leads across some green, and regularly manured, pasture westwards to a gate, then through a series of gateways in transverse walls which separate fields of increasingly rough pasture. This is, however, a good firm trod, with no doubts at all as to its direction and, on leaving the metal gate through the highest wall with open moor beyond, a clearly distinguishable path of pocket-steps leads up the last steep slope to a large stone pillar on the shoulder of the moor above.

Pillars of stones, as opposed to cairns (which are really just heaps of stones) are frequently known as 'beacons' because they can be seen across large distances and are the site for signals of some kind or other. In the past, of course, as when the Spanish Armada was sighted sailing up the Channel in 1588, these signals were bonfires, lit

The 'Pile of Stones' on Penhill ➤

on the spot so that as many people as possible would know of the event. This particular pile of stones is unusual in that it is not the normal slender, tapering shape, like a
candle, but is more like a tall square box, with one side collapsing. It looks a bit like a
horse without legs, with a neck but no head. The OS map is confusing in this
respect because, in antique lettering, it marks something called 'Penhill Beacon'
about 150 yds north-west of the 'Pile of Stones'.

Walking in that direction (north-west) which is, in fact, along the edge of the
escarpment, you reach in about 150 yds a stony mound just back from the edge of
the drop, where the first small gritstone crag outcrops. This is the site of 'Penhill
Beacon' and it was certainly the place used for the VE Day celebration bonfire in
the summer of 1995, because I saw the embers myself. It is supposed also to be the
site of an Iron Age chieftain's burial mound. The only thing wrong with it as a 'beacon' is that you cannot distinguish the actual site from a distance unless there is a
bonfire there, whereas the 'Pile of Stones' is visible for miles.

Continue along the edge on a grassy path for another 150 yds or so until you reach
a wall, crossed by a slit-stile; beyond this are the first sizeable outcrops of steep rock.
This is Penhill Scar. An obvious path continues along the edge, to the north of the
substantial wall on the left.

On the other side of this wall is a large area of almost level moor which, apart from being used for grouse-shooting, also shelters numerous species of moorland birds. A YDNP notice mentions that lapwing, golden plover, redshank, ring ouzel and curlew are all found up here. They need all the protection they can get, especially in the breeding season (April to June), *so please do not cross this wall*; you will anyway only make it much more difficult for yourself to find the way off the steep ground ahead.

Walkers closely following the OS map will by now be aware that the route is not on anything which corresponds to the public bridleway, which is shown on the map (and, in fact, not traceable on the ground anyway) as running onto the top of Penhill and coming to a dead end on the grouse moor. The way described, for which I have to thank Mr H. T. Thornton-Berry of Swinithwaite who was most helpful in this matter, avoids the grouse moor by keeping to the north side of the bounding wall and then chooses the best possible way to link up with the public footpath shown on the map immediately north of Black Scar. There is, in fact, no sign of that path either on the ground in its higher reaches, but lower down it shows as a deep groove slanting across the fellside, from Black Scar to Penhill Quarry (disused) and continu-

ing to Flint Lane; it was obviously used by the quarrymen extracting stone. So please bear with me. The route sounds complicated but is in fact very straightforward.

The good path runs along the top of Penhill Scar, which has a great mass of boulders in the hollow at its foot, and allows splendid long-distance views up and across Wensleydale. The trig point may be spotted just peeping over the wall when the wall itself is about 40 yds away from the edge, but then the wall creeps closer and closer to the edge until there is only about 5 yds between them. Here, in the gap between wall and edge, a bit of wire fencing was once in place but there is a clear gap now between fence and wall and the path continues through it. Beyond this gap the path splits into several less obvious trods as walkers (and sheep, no doubt) have sought their way forward. Continue in the generally western direction along the edge, but it now fades and what was a distinct escarpment simply becomes steep ground.

Some 200–300 yds before reaching the next escarpment, Black Scar – and this is the important part – *before reaching it*, turn half-right downhill on this convex slope to the north-west and, although you cannot initially see it, you will intersect with a very obvious deep-cut grassy groove which has clearly been man-made. This slants

Below Penhill, looking west

◄ *Looking west along Penhill Scar, Wensleydale below*

back, half-right, in the opposite direction to which you have been walking. Follow this downhill to the north-east, towards the caravans that you should be able to see in Chantry Park in the valley bottom. As it gets below the steepest ground, this groove turns back sharp left (WNW) and leads further downhill onto the flatter moor. If you fail to find this deep groove, just go down the rough ground *heading north-west* towards the more level ground below, obviously avoiding any rocky outcrops as you do. But I will be surprised if you fail to spot the groove. There are numerous old and grassed-over spoil-tips down at this level, remains of the ancient Penhill Quarry workings, and here this grooved path again turns right (north-east) towards a gate in a distant field corner, but follow it now for only 50 yds or so to a cairn just past a spoil-tip.

The central part of the rough pasture below was at one time divided into fields by stone walls, but these have all been collapsed for many years (shown on the OS map by dotted straight lines rather than solid ones). The area as a whole is, however, enclosed by solid walls so you now need to swing *north-west again* and follow a faint trod, with a couple of cairns, across the pasture (and one of these collapsed walls) to find a gate in the lower enclosing wall (grid ref 043873, the nearest wall corner is about 120 yds away on your left). A Yorkshire Dales National Park notice on its other side asks you to ensure that you close it, so once you find that you can be certain that you are in the right place. (Look back from here to Penhill and the zigzag way down the concave fellside between Penhill Scar and Black Scar will be perfectly obvious.)

A grassy track leads away left from this gate but quickly curves downhill and to the right, passing a 'footpath' finger-post, and turns below a small limestone escarpment to reach a gateway with a wicket-gate beside it. Go through this and curve left on a distinct track which within 50 yds becomes a green groove (Stony Gate) leading directly to a gateway on High Lane. A walled lane (leading to Nossill End, Nossill Bank, Green Gate and West Witton) is directly opposite, but is *not* the way to go.

Bad-weather alternative route, avoiding Penhill

Walkers who find themselves approaching Penhill in deteriorating weather, perhaps with mist beginning to cloud the highest tops, may avoid the climb up to Penhill by taking an interesting traversing line instead. For this, instead of turning uphill on the Melmerby–Carlton road on arrival at Penhill Farm, they should go straight across the road at the junction (immediately right of the farm buildings) to enter the narrow walled Flint Lane, heading west (finger-post 'FP Penhill Quarry 1'). In 100 yds this pleasant track turns sharp left, then sharp right in a further 100 yds. After that it continues traversing, with attractive views over the valley on the right below. Just over 1 mile after leaving Penhill Farm, the walls come to an end where it turns into a huge field, whose slopes rise on the left (south) up to Penhill Crags, Penhill Scar and Black Scar, with the old spoil-tips of the disused Penhill Quarry very obvious on the lower slopes.

Continue traversing along a grassy track for about 700 yds, with the wall on your immediate right all the time, until it is pierced by a gate. Turn right through this, spotting a YDNP notice on its other side asking that you close it. Here you are at grid ref 043873, the nearest wall corner is about 120 yds away to the west and you have rejoined the main high-level route.

High Lane to Aysgarth via the Templars Chapel

High Lane is typical of many green roads in the Dales. It runs along a well-drained and almost level limestone shelf, walled on both sides but with eight to ten feet of grassy space on each side of the central tractor track so that it gives pleasant walking underfoot.

Stone sarcophagi at the Penhill Preceptory

Turn left (west) along High Lane for almost ½ mile, until it reaches a dip, after which there is another, but narrower, walled lane on the right. Turn right along this for 200 yds to where it bends to the right, with a roofless barn on the corner and a small disused quarry on the left. The track is concreted here as it goes down a bank (another limestone shelf) to one level terrace and then, having crossed it, down another. Halfway down this second concrete strip you will see a finger-post reading 'FP Nossill Ln 1 via Langthwaite Lane', then the concrete strip curves left and then sharply back right. On this last sharp bend leave the track for a grassy path heading (left) west which leads downhill across pasture, with walls and woods on each side so that you are funnelled towards a gate in the bottom corner. Beyond this gate, a track leads down another easy slope onto another wide grassy limestone shelf and towards the fenced-off area of the enigmatic Penhill Preceptory.

Here a notice reads: 'These walls and graves belonged to a Chapel in a Preceptory of the Knights Templar, built in about 1200 and handed over, on their suppression in 1312, to the Hospitallers. The Chapel, the remains of which were uncovered in 1840, served adjoining residential buildings that have not been exposed.' The Knights Templar were the most powerful of the three great military orders which emerged out of the extraordinary episodes of the Crusades, the other two being the Knights of St John of Jerusalem and the Teutonic Order of St Mary, although the latter had neither houses nor members in the British Isles. According to my dictionary, a 'preceptory' was a subordinate community.

What catches the attention immediately are the three stone sarcophagi, with heavy stone lids just laid to one side, and one immediately thinks that each one of these must have held the corpse of an important person, for the inner shape of each sarcophagus is roughly that of a human body, with a shape for a head and a trunk. The fact that the notice mentions 'graves' encourages this supposition. But on a little more reflection, the two smaller of these stone 'coffins' look more like keyholes and far too small to have contained human corpses since, although they are about 4 ft 6 ins long, they are only about 9 ins wide at the widest point. The biggest coffin could conceivably have held a corpse, although its length is only just over 5 ft. I conclude that if these sarcophagi held human remains, then either thirteenth-century Knights Templar were very tiny (and too unbelievably tiny to have worn the armour and carried the swords that we know they did carry) or they were for some other purpose.

Leaving the Preceptory, tranquil but for the sheep munching the grass and the rooks cawing in the nearby trees, a narrow slit-stile leads through the wall and into a rough walled lane, with a sign 'FP Temple Farm ¼'. Turning right and left, the lane immediately becomes a rough track slanting down beneath trees overhanging the track to a gate at the bottom of the slope, then swings right down a muddy track towards Temple Farm, distinguished by a huge silage tower and a mound of silage covered in black plastic and old tyres, reaching a slit-stile onto the main A684.

Turn left here and, with care for this is a busy road, walk down the hill on the right-hand verge, past the junction with the B6160, to cross Walden Beck at Hestholme Bridge. (At this point, the main route from Wensley Bridge and Redmire Force joins.)

On the far side of the bridge, a finger-post on the right at the entrance to the drive to Hestholme Farm points across level pasture towards the River Ure, which can now be heard, if not yet seen. Two wicket-gates lead to the river bank, close by a series of small cascades where the river flows over some small steps in the underlying limestone pavement. Just ahead you can see that the river emerges from a vertically sided rock gorge and, although the OS map shows the path splitting, with one branch going along the bank, it is in fact channelled by a fence so it climbs up the slope above and to the left of the gorge, probably to avoid the risk of accidents. Aysgarth Falls' Lower Force can be seen, but only partly, as it is screened by trees.

The path rises further away from the bank and you will only get a glimpse of the majestic Middle Force, the most dramatic stretch of the River Ure in Wensleydale, so you must make a firm resolution to cross to the other bank for a good view before leaving Aysgarth; it is worth it. In the meantime, the path continues through a small sycamore plantation, emerging on the edge of a field directly opposite the noble building of St Andrew's Church, Aysgarth.

The path leads directly into and through the church grounds. Reaching the road, a left turn leads uphill to the Youth Hostel and the village, for accommodation. A right turn leads downhill to cross the river by Yore Bridge to view the spectacular falls.

See pages 14–16 for information about the splendid places of interest that Aysgarth has to offer.

Day Two

Aysgarth to Hawes

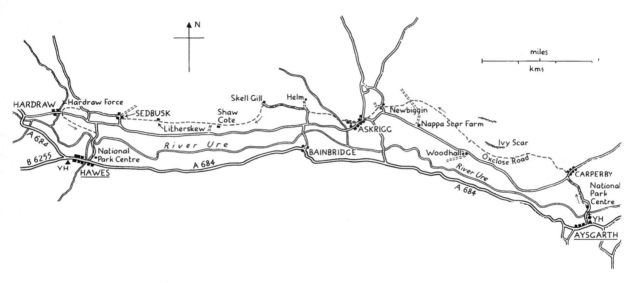

➤ *Distance:* About 12½ miles/20km
➤ *Altitude gained:* About 575 ft/175 m
➤ *Terrain:* Occasionally muddy but generally on good and well-drained paths.
➤ *Refreshments:* Plenty of choice in Askrigg, also in Hardraw.

The second stage of the walk transfers to the north side of Wensleydale and is generally along a series of broad limestone shelves or terraces at approximately mid-height along the valley side. Compared to the intimate riverside scenery of yesterday on the low-level walk from Wensley Bridge to Aysgarth, the views to be enjoyed today are much more open, for the river is below the line of sight and is therefore only noticed occasionally. But, like yesterday, once a little initial height is gained, the walking is generally on the level and on firm ground: no slutchy morasses or bogs to cope with yet. Route-finding is reasonably straightforward; there should be no more than two or three places where doubt may arise and I have taken particular care to try to highlight these in the text.

◄ *Aysgarth High Force*

This second day's walking goes via Hardraw Force to Hawes. Hardraw Force is the longest unbroken waterfall above ground in England and really must be seen in person to appreciate; the finest photograph can only give a rough idea of the height and beauty of this remarkable cascade. Since the third day of this walk (which has a high-level variation), from Hawes to Kirkby Stephen, is also the longest, an early start will be advisable. It is therefore sensible to view Hardraw Force *today*, if at all possible; you may well be in too much of a rush to see it at all in the morning. You don't want to return home and have family and friends say, incredulously: 'You went to Hardraw and didn't go and look at Hardraw Force!'

While on the topic of waterfalls, if, when you reached Aysgarth the previous day, you did not have a look at Aysgarth's equally famous cascades, you have a last opportunity to do so this morning, by making a slight diversion from the route of the walk.

Aysgarth to Carperby

From Aysgarth village or the Youth Hostel, return towards and continue past the entrance to St Andrew's Church, continuing downhill on the well-signed road towards Aysgarth Falls and Carperby. This road winds quite steeply round a bend to Yore Bridge, with the sound of the rushing waters very evident for some time before you can actually see them. Rounding the bend you can see High Force over the wall on the left.

On the north side of Yore Bridge turn left through a kissing-gate. Ignore the sign for the picnic area and also that reading 'FP Askrigg 4 miles' because, although one of today's intermediate destinations is Askrigg, the footpath is at a low level and much of it along or beside the former Wensleydale Railway. It is easy going but, after a fairly short distance, also very boring. Instead, take the tarmac footpath signed for 'National Park Centre' which points right and rises gently away from the road. In 100 yds it passes the centre's car park, on the right, but do not enter it.

(If you wish to view the Middle or Lower Forces, you *should* enter here and you will find signs to the viewing points at the exit from the car park, turning right down the road and then almost immediately left through a gate. A visit will probably take you about 20 minutes, or less, but then return.)

Climb some steps up to the banking above the end of the car park and cross over it to descend to a metal kissing-gate. As you do, you will realise that you have just crossed what must have been another part of the Wensleydale Railway, closed down in the famous Dr Beeching's era. Sprouting vegetation and well-established trees are

Typical Dales barn seen on the approach to Carperby ➤

rapidly smothering the track here; in other places, it is simply a grassy embankment. From the kissing-gate, the path leads north to a stile, crossing a fenced meadow to another stile, then slightly right across another field towards a gate with two stone gate-posts (which leads onto the road). Don't go through it but shadow the wall on your right to reach a slit-stile further on and here you should debouch onto the road.

As you walk through these fields and come over the rise you will see the barns and houses of Carperby, and realise that the skyline ahead is formed by limestone scars. The way ahead will prove to be towards these, turning left (west) just below them.

Having now joined the tarmac, you will very likely spot a 'footpath' sign on the right that appears to cut a corner into Carperby village. Resist the temptation, for this becomes a very messy alternative, crossing what looks like a slurry drain at one point and dodging multiple cow-flops in a farm yard at another. Much better to just stay on the tarmac for a short distance, turning right into Carperby.

Here your attention will be caught by the stone cross on the wedge-shaped village green, with a large sycamore at the narrow end. It stands on a square base which has seven tiers, each smaller than the one below. The date 1674 is carved on the cross itself, with a rather lugubrious face carved on the end of each cross piece. It is difficult now to imagine that this sleepy little village once had an important Dales market, its market charter dating from as long ago as 1305. I don't think you

can even buy an ice-cream there now. And whereas many Dales villages have Wesleyan Chapels, Carperby was also once an important centre for Quakerism. If you turn left (west) from the cross, along the green, you will pass the largest building in Carperby which is indeed the Friends Meeting House (1874). Just past it is a Wesleyan Chapel with the date 1890 on it and just past that again is a smaller building, now a private house, which has a plaque on it reading 'Wesleyan Methodist Chapel erected 1820'. It is obvious that the small chapel became too small and the larger one took over.

Carperby to Askrigg

At the west end of the green (where you entered the village), look for a double finger-post. The finger you need points north-west and reads 'To other paths ½ mile'. Follow this, then in 50 yds there is another finger-post and a wicket-gate with the sign 'Oxclose'; this is a comfort because, even though it looks as if you are being directed into a cow-floppy farm yard, you can see a stile over a wall directly ahead. Go past the entrance to a shippon to the stile which leads into an enclosed, grassy wide lane rising up the slope beyond.

At the gateway at the head of this lane, bear left (west) following orange paint blobs to a slit-stile leading onto a farm track. Turn right (NW) up this, towards the line of limestone scars ahead, following it to a metal gate at the top of a slight bend, where this track intersects with another. Turn left here, climbing slightly, and in about 150 yds you will pass through an old quarry where some huge Yoredale slabs, looking as though they have been there a century at least, are piled up on the left. There is a deep cave excavated into the gritstone below a limestone layer on the right, which is probably where the slabs came from. There is a good view from here looking back over Carperby to Penhill in the south-east.

A pleasant grass track now curves onto the green and grassy top of the limestone layer, turns left through a gateway and into a large field. Tractor tracks confuse things somewhat, but there is only one gateway in the wall across your line of march westwards and beyond it lies a lovely green way, stretching enticingly along a level shelf below gleaming limestone scars. You are now on what the OS map names 'Oxclose Road (Path)' and you can stride out confidently. The sharp neb of Addlebrough, on the other side of Wensleydale, is now directly in your line of sight ahead. The green track soon skirts round the edge of an area of exposed ground where the little mounds of spoil are all that is left of a former lead mine; three or four adits can be seen driven into the fellside a little higher up.

Looking over Wensleydale towards Penhill from above Carperby ➤

On the far side of the old mine floor, the green track becomes more like a jeep track, leading to a gate and ford over the narrow Thackthwaite Beck, crossing it immediately upstream of a little waterfall tumbling over a limestone lip. Follow the track and turn with it through a gate in the wall on the left (ignoring a track shown on the OS map which does not go through the gate but makes for Beldhaw Hill). Beyond the gate the track turns downhill towards the village of Woodhall, but follow it for only 10 yds or so and then turn back sharp right (north-west) and climb the slope on an obvious track heading for a gateway seen ahead. After that tricky little bit, the way ahead is now perfectly obvious again, even though it is very rutted for a few hundred yards until you reach some sheep pens and dipping tanks and a sign 'Danger Sheep Dip'. From what I have read the stuff is lethal.

With the Ure seen winding in lazy meanders below, the path now continues along more delightful close-cropped grassy terrain, along the top edge of a little mixed plantation, passing a finger-post, pointing backwards, that indicates 'BW Castle Bolton 5'. This lovely green sward continues along a level shelf, below the conifer plantation of The Coombs seen up above, until you are almost below Ellerkin Scar. At a gate beside a barn, the path runs into a walled lane. From here you look down to the warm grey stone houses and square church tower of Askrigg while, looking

half-left across the valley, you can see the walled lane of the Cam High Road, straight as a legionary's sword, rising out of Bainbridge which was once the site of a Roman garrison.

Go down this walled lane, ignoring a metalled turn off left which leads to Nappa Scar Farm, and in about 100 yds turn left through a slit-stile towards a mixed wood just down the slope. Nappa Scar Farm, incidentally, is just above Nappa Hall, once owned by Sir Christopher Metcalfe, who was visited by Mary Queen of Scots for two days while she was a 'prisoner' at Bolton Castle; her ghost is reputed to have been frequently seen here. The tower of the hall, a good example of a mid-fifteenth-century pele tower, may just be glimpsed through the trees.

The path slants through the wood, which has lots of bluebells in May and early June, then keeps to the top side of the farm buildings beyond to a slit-stile, across the next two fields by two more stiles, turns alongside a wall to a fourth and then slants across a pasture into the hamlet of Newbiggin. Pass between the houses and take the track ahead, beyond the tiny green, past a building beside the beck and which was probably once the local mill. Follow the walled lane ahead for about 70 yds and then, just before reaching a gate into a field, turn left through a slit-stile onto a path heading south-west across a meadow towards a barn. A stile next to the barn and then more stiles lead fairly steeply to the south-west down Stony Bank to reach a metalled road just north of Askrigg.

I sat down on a wooden seat here and started to eat my sandwiches, but a horse tethered nearby soon discovered that its rope was sufficiently long to get close enough to pester me for titbits so I had to move on or risk going hungry. Downhill leads into Askrigg; turn right towards Hawes when you reach the Leyburn–Hawes road and enter the market place.

This has a cobbled area, a village cross similar to, but later than, that at Carperby, a village pump, an iron bull-ring (although this is often hidden beneath a parked car) and quite a few three-storey buildings. These are unusual in the Dales and give an indication of the solid prosperity that was the norm here for many centuries. Only recently I was reading that archaeologists are to dig up the market place to find traces of an historical toll booth that is known to have existed there. In the early nineteenth century, this building was used to house carts, a part was leased to church wardens to accommodate hearses and there was a vagrants' room. Askrigg undoubtedly has an air of tradition and continuity with the past, and the massive buttresses and crenellated roofline of the ancient St Oswald's Church emphasise it. On the notice board outside the church there is an added note reading: 'N. Pevsner wrote: "The best Tudor roof in the North Riding."' Pevsner was absolutely right and nobody could deny that the huge roof beams are superb, so don't just rush past but take a look inside this lovely building. Needless to say, there is plenty of refreshment and accommodation to be found here if needed.

Askrigg: the pump, the cross and St Oswald's Church

◄ *Askrigg, with Addlebrough beyond*

Askrigg to Skell Gill

Looking from the market place to the right (north) of the church is a metalled road and sign 'Footpath Mill Gill Force'. Go along this until it shortly becomes a gravel track, turning off it to the right just before the entrance to Mill Gill House. Here follows a causeway of stone flags across the edge of a buttercup meadow towards Mill Gill and the old mill buildings. Passing beneath its former aqueduct (it functioned as a mill until 1890) to a narrow footbridge over the heavily wooded gill, the path leads to the right up the left edge of the gill. In early summer the air is heavy with the scent of ramsons here, for they cover the bank below the path for quite a distance. After about 300 yds, look down into the gill to spot an almost overgrown building beside the stream. This housed a turbine and was the source of Askrigg's electricity supply until it joined the National Grid in 1948.

Reaching a junction of paths, there is a finger-post for Whitfield Gill (which is straight ahead) and for Mill Gill (for which you fork right). In my opinion, unless there has been a lot of water recently, Whitfield Gill is hardly worth the effort needed to reach it, but Mill Gill is close at hand (only 200 yds or so away), where there is a 30-ft (I guess) cascade into a fine amphitheatre.

Retracing steps from the waterfall, continue up the left bank of the gill (as if for

Whitfield Gill) but in about 100 yds turn off left at a finger-post signed 'FP Helm ½' going left at a slit-stile and away from the gill. (This sign is slightly misleading in that the path does not go directly to Helm, a house, but to the bottom of its drive.) Go west up a slope (no clear path) close to the wall and, in that same line when it comes to an end, cross a last bit of open pasture to reach a junction of tarmac roads: you are now at the end of the drive to Helm. Go straight across the junction and into Skell Gill Lane, heading due west. This is an almost level tarmac-surfaced minor road which passes Lukes House on the left and then ends in the little hamlet of Skell Gill.

Skell Gill to Sedbusk

Going through Skell Gill, you cross a hump bridge over a little stream, then pass a house with an outbuilding on which is a delightful white-painted dovecot, with white doves popping their heads in and out of the little pigeon-holes, which are individually named 'Titch' and 'Flapper' above.

The tarmac ends just after the last house, but continue ahead into a walled lane with two bends, keeping left on the main track when it forks just before a little ford. You remain in a walled lane for another 100 yds to a gate beside some sheep pens and go up the slope beyond, now with the wall on your left only. At the top of the slope, the track you are on swings left at the wall corner but here you must turn half-right (south-west) across pasture, with no clear sign of a path initially but very quickly reaching a lovely green way just above a wall running west.

The way ahead is now straightforward again for about 1½ miles but underfoot it slowly changes from grass to gravelled farm track. You pass a few barns and then farm buildings at Shaw Cote, where there is a finger-post at the exit from the farm reading 'Sedbusk 1½ miles'. Just beyond Shaw Cote

The packhorse bridge in the hamlet of Skell Gill

◄ *From Skell Gill Lane, looking across Wensleydale to Addlebrough* the way leads into a walled lane and after about 150 yds along this and just before a bend to the left, take a stile on the right (with a gate beside it). This leads you to another lovely grass footpath which can be seen continuing west through a line of slit-stiles, with traditional barns, ubiquitous ash trees and, at least in summer, buttercups and clover giving the fields both colour and heavenly fragrance.

There is an art in getting your body through some of these stiles. A few of them have little gates across the slit between the stones; this is usually when the slit alone is wide enough to allow lambs to squeeze through, but when the spring on the gate is a strong one it can cause the gate to give you a crack on the ankle as you try to squeeze through before it shuts. Some of the narrow ones are too tight to get my boot through (I admit to big feet and size 13 boots so you may think it is not surprising) and then I have to do a bit of leg-waving and balancing on my hands. My dog Henry is facing a small weight challenge and he has a struggle too, usually solved by being hauled into the air by the scruff of his neck and dumped without ceremony on the other side. Stiles, however, are comforting; they indicate that you are on the path.

The last slit-stile leads to the hamlet of Litherskew, where there are three or four buildings and a circular walled grass enclosure. You may dither a little here, but take

the most direct line possible between the buildings ahead (i.e. first slightly right and then slightly left after the last slit-stile). This will lead to a slit-stile seen ahead just to the left of a collapsed building and then the way is clear again: more delightful meadows full of clover, vetches, buttercups, cow parsley, daisies, all crossed via a line of slit-stiles leading to Sedbusk. On the approach, when there is a choice of ways, keep left to a slit-stile leading into a narrow strip of mature trees. The path leads through this, emerging to continue with the wall on your right and into Sedbusk

Sedbusk to Hardraw

On entering Sedbusk from Litherskew the path leads in front of several cottages and reaches a tarmac road. Join this, bearing slightly right then, with Rose Cottage and then Nether House on your right-hand side, continue going west into the narrow walled and metalled Sedbusk Lane. At its end, it curves downhill slightly to a junction with another road, the one running between Wensleydale and Swaledale via the Butter Tubs Pass.

Go straight across at the junction to a finger-post signed 'FP Hardraw ¼'. A narrow footpath now leads through a belt of woodland on a banking below the level of the road which is now up above on your right. It leaves the wood by a stile, crossing more open ground to another stile from where the church of St John and St Mary and the village of Hardraw come into view. An obvious trod leads towards these across sheep pasture, via one more stile, curving left on the final approach to Hardraw and reaching the road between two buildings. An immediate right turn here puts you outside the premises of the Green Dragon Inn, through which you enter to view Hardraw Force.

It is, of course, the existence of Hardraw Force that makes the little village of Hardraw such an attraction. This is a real waterfall, not just a cascade splashing down a high cliff, touching it at many points on its descent. Here the waters take a 100-ft leap into space, over the rim of a fine wooded amphitheatre, and its leap is so extravagant that it is possible to actually walk behind the cataract without getting wet. Entrance to the amphitheatre is through the premises of the Green Dragon pub (small entrance charge) and then a short walk leads directly to the base of the falls. It is truly a sight not to be missed.

The acoustics of the amphitheatre are so good, and the Wensleydale Railway made Hawes so accessible, that it was used for brass band contests from 1881 onwards. With a few interruptions, these were held here until the Second World War but that and the closure of the railway brought them to an end until the present proprietors,

◄ *Looking east from near Sedbusk, a typical Dales meadow*

in 1989, revived them again. So the second Sunday in September each year since then has seen the Yorkshire and Humberside Brass Band Association making the cliffs resound again. Long may it continue.

Hardraw to Hawes

Leaving the Green Dragon, cross the road towards the tea shop opposite (itself worth a little diversion) and, at the right-hand side of the building, look for a finger-post, beside a gate and stile, reading 'FP Brunt Acres Road (Pennine Way)'. This is the start of the path to Hawes and, within a few yards, another finger-post ('P. W.') points to the left (south-east). A narrow causeway of stone flags now leads beside the wall on the left, away from some farm buildings and then across sheep pastures, providing an unmistakable way forward. The flags remain until you have passed through three gates and when they come to an end, an obvious trod continues through more fields, with a few more stiles, soon leading down some steps onto Brunt Acres Road.

Turn right here along the road to cross the River Ure by the attractive Haylands Bridge on the approach to Hawes; on the far side of the bridge watch for a path on the right, signed for the Pennine Way which, via more stone flags, leads into Hawes.

Hawes is the highest market town in Yorkshire, an important agricultural centre for the Dales, with busy livestock auctions on Tuesdays and Saturdays and a stroll around it reveals many things of interest. A sign carved in the stone over the doorway of Cockett's Hotel by the market place reads 'God being with us who can be against'. There is not even a question mark. It is a sentiment of confidence that is almost palpably felt here; perhaps it is to do with the bracing air at this slightly higher altitude. Here also is the Board Hotel and when I passed through last time I was greatly taken by a notice in the window which read: 'Lunch: Yorkshire Trencher. A very large Yorkshire Pudding filled to overflowing with roast beef, choice of potatoes and vegetables of the day. For large appetites only. £4.95.' That seemed like real good Yorkshire value to me.

But it is not just local farmers who come to Hawes. I chatted to three people in the market place, all waiting for a bus. They were three independent American visitors. I didn't manage to find out much more about them because I was too fascinated by the silver ring with a lump on it that one of the Americans, a girl aged about twenty, had through her *eyebrow*, for Heaven's sake. It looked sore and inflamed and I can't say I was surprised.

A school party below Hardraw Force ➤

Hawes has for many years been known as the centre for the production of Wensleydale cheese and it caused great consternation when the Wensleydale Dairy producing it was closed in 1992 by its parent company, as part of a rationalisation plan. This not only destroyed the jobs of people whose families had been living in the dale for centuries but there was an added insult that Wensleydale cheese looked

as if it was going to be produced in, of all places, Lancashire. Happily, although only after many palpitations, the local management secured the necessary backing to re-start and there is now a Wensleydale Creamery in business again producing that delicious cheese. (Let us hope that the bureaucrats of Brussels don't notice or they will surely look for some excuse to close it down.) The opportunity was also taken to create a museum, a restaurant and bar, and a produce and souvenir shop. It is very interesting, well signed and found just on the west edge of town. The Visitor Centre offers a tour called 'The Cheese Experience' although the best time for seeing cheesemaking is between 10.30 a.m. and 3 p.m. The Centre itself is open Monday to Saturday 9.30 a.m. to 5 p.m.

Hawes is the last settlement of any size in Wensleydale. Beyond it lie the high moors of the Pennines and the way over to Mallerstang and Kirkby Stephen. Walkers who, for whatever reason, find that they need to shorten the walk as a whole, may consider the Short Cut to Swaledale via the Pennine Way over Great Shunner Fell. This is most specifically *not* a recommendation, as it will omit some of the best scenery and terrain, nor is it an escape route in the event of bad weather: the weather on Great Shunner Fell is not likely to be any better than that on Wild Boar Fell. However, for any walker who has good reason to use this Short Cut, the details will be found on page 118.

The busy main street of Hawes

Day Three

Hawes to Kirkby Stephen

continued p. 54

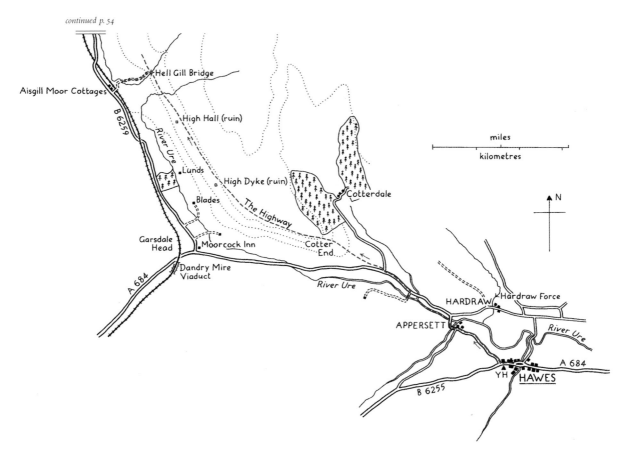

- ➤ *Distance:* About 15½ miles/24.8km on main route; about 19½ miles/ 31.2km on high-level variation
- ➤ *Altitude gained:* About 850 ft/259m on main route; about 2350 ft/716m on high-level variation
- ➤ *Terrain:* A bit of tarmac, otherwise grassy paths, mostly along high-level limestone shelves. (On the high-level variation there are sometimes boggy slopes to gain the high land, after which the going is good.)
- ➤ *Refreshments:* It is advisable to carry supplies with you although there are lunch-time possibilities at The Thrang. (On the high-level variation there is a good tea-room/café at Aisgill Moor Cottages.)

Barns and fields outside Hawes, looking west ➤

The third stage of this walk crosses from Wensleydale to Mallerstang, the valley of the upper Eden. Both the main route and the high-level variation walk over the same ground as far as Hell Gill Bridge. Here the main route continues traversing and then gently descends into the Mallerstang valley. The high-level variation, for those who feel fit enough to tackle the extra 4 miles/6.4km and 1500 ft/457m of altitude, begins at Hell Gill Bridge (*see* page 65).

Apart from the first ½-mile on the A684 leaving Hawes, this is also when the change is made from the Wensleydale map (OS Outdoor Leisure 30) to the Howgill Fells and Upper Eden Valley map (OS Outdoor Leisure 19).

The first part of the day's walking being therefore common to both means that you will have an opportunity to assess all the relevant conditions of weather, fitness or inclination before committing yourself to the greater heights of Swarth Fell and Wild Boar Fell on the high-level variation.

Hawes to Cotter End

From Hawes take the main road (A684) for Kirkby Stephen and head north-west, crossing the dismantled Wensleydale railway again, and staying with the road to

where it kinks over Widdale Beck in the village of Appersett. On a slight descent just after leaving Hawes for Appersett, look beyond the walled fields and barns and you will get a view up Cotterdale. Its lower flanks and the valley bottom are draped in conifer forest but the two enclosing ridges rise above the forestry. The right-hand one sweeps northwards and rises to the high gritstone moorland of Great Shunner Fell and is used by the Pennine Way; this is the "short-cut route' to Swaledale (*see* page 118). The left-hand one climbs to the north-east and shows the line of today's walk, the Highway.

As soon as you have crossed Widdale Beck, look for a footpath on the left side of the road (signed for 'Mossdale Head') which it shadows as far as New Bridge, where the A684 crosses the River Ure again. Now the path runs beside the river, on its south bank, keeping close to a narrow belt of woodland fringing it. It passes through this strip and, having crossed two more pastures, reaches a farm track. Turn right here to rejoin the main road in 100 yds and then turn left along the A684 again. Gaining height gradually, in about ½ mile you reach the point where a minor road turns off to the right, signed for 'Cotterdale only' as it is a cul-de-sac.

Here, on this corner, is a finger-post reading 'Lady Anne Clifford's Highway' and pointing directly up the spur of the ridge ahead (north-west). The faint path, found on the left as soon as you have crossed the cattle-grid where this minor road joins the A684, runs initially over coarse grass and close to the main road, which is over the wall on the left, but soon parts company with it as the road turns west towards Garsdale Head. The path climbs steadily along the crest of the broad ridge, soon accompanied by a solid wall, to pass through a gate at a transverse wall just below the brow of the ridge. Above the gate, the angle steepens quite sharply, but only for a short way for, here on Cotter End (the name presumably referring to the steep blunt end of the ridge), it soon eases and becomes a green path, with a wall on its left side, striding along the top edge of a fine escarpment.

Cotter End to Hell Gill Bridge

Almost at the top of this last uphill pull you pass a large lime-kiln, set below what looks like an old quarry. To the right of the kiln and just above it is a comfortable bench-seat, with a bird's eye view back towards Wensleydale, a handy place for a short breather. The plaque on the seat commemorates a 'trail-rider' who 'found neutral at last' and the tyre-marks nearby suggest that he was probably a motor-bike rider. Thank goodness the 'trail' up here is over very firm ground, sometimes bare rock, so that tyre-marks are not particularly destructive of the surface. Indeed the

On Lady Anne Clifford's Highway, beyond Cotter End ➤

'trail', the Highway, now becomes a splendid green track marching along an almost level sill or plateau of limestone. The limestone outcropping here is one of the reasons why the lime-kiln is here also, but not the only one.

The way is now along a green path, with a wall on its left side, striding along the top edge of a fine escarpment. As you now strike out along this splendid path it will soon be apparent that there are higher heather slopes and peat groughs on the right, clearly showing that the limestone shelf is overlaid by higher gritstone strata. Although it will not be seen from this path, because you are at a higher level, a journey by car after heavy rain along the B6259 road which runs through the Mallerstang valley will occasionally allow you to see where great cascades of water suddenly spout out of holes as if by magic on the steep fellside. This is caused by the run-off of water from the higher and impermeable gritstone layer above the Highway disappearing down sinkholes as soon as it reaches the limestone layer, vanishing underground and then re-appearing as it reaches gritstone again. One of these, above Hanging Lund, can reappear with great violence and I have seen it in a high wind, when the waters were being blown back up the fellside like a plume of smoke from a chimney.

The lime-kiln just passed is a good example of many which still exist in most parts of the limestone Dales but it is probably at least a century since any of them were used for their original purpose. Like the walls which parcel up the fields and lend such distinctive character to the landscape, it is easy to take them for granted. Looking like low square or round towers, each with an arch at its base, which may also be either round or square or 'gothic', they played an important role in improving poor or 'sour' land as it was increasingly realised that lime derived from raw limestone was not only useful for producing mortar for building but as a fertiliser. The process was known as early as the thirteenth century, although the use was greatly extended from the seventeenth century onwards.

Essentially, the kiln worked by being built rather like a square or circular hopper out of pieces of limestone, the sides tapering from an open mouth at the top to a narrow opening at the bottom, with access to this by way of the arch. The 'hopper' was filled from the top with alternate layers of pieces of limestone and combustible materials such as coal or wood. Then a fire lit at the bottom and fanned by the draught up the 'chimney' formed by the sides of the kiln would break down the limestone, firstly into small pieces and then into a white powder. This was raked out at the bottom and placed on the fields in small heaps and left to slake in the weather. The amount of labour involved in this was, of course, prodigious but the availability of both limestone and the materials to burn it were crucial.

Fortunately the Yoredale Series of rocks often has a thin seam of coal just below the gritstone layer, with the limestones just below that, so the lime-kilns for local use were often built at the upper limit of a farmer's fields. It only needed a ratio of 1:4 coal to limestone, so coal could be carried downhill to the kilns which were themselves placed on the limestone strata. The lime itself was then carried downhill to the fields. Incidentally, breaking up the limestone contributed to the formation of the terraces that line so many of the valley sides and contribute so much to the appearance of the landscape. Coal in small but efficient quantities to work this particular kiln here on Cotter End must have been found when it was needed in the past.

It is easy going along this green track on the edge of the escarpment, with a good view across the intervening couple of miles on the left to Dandry Mire Viaduct at the head of Garsdale. The famous Settle–Carlisle railway line crosses this and through the gap at Garsdale Head then turns north, still climbing, to its highest point on Aisgill Moor. Our line of march runs parallel to it, through an almost treeless landscape apart from a stand of sitka spruce at Lunds and the few trees that shelter individual farmsteads.

About ¼ mile along this green track, the path begins to gently decline downhill, but it is not until you have passed through a gate at a transverse wall and then gone another ½ mile or so that you see ahead the ruins of High Dyke. It is difficult to believe now, when you look down to the road and railway far below, that in the late eighteenth and early nineteenth centuries this was once an important drove road for cattle being brought to markets in England from Scotland. High Dyke was a pub or inn built to catch the drovers' custom. Now all you will find are collapsing roofs and sheep droppings and if you fancy a drink here you will need to either have a hip flask or have poured a dram into your coffee thermos.

About a mile beyond High Dyke, having crossed the course of several little gills en route, you pass more ruins, this time those of High Hall. Approximately ½ mile further, still walking on firm springy grass on these slightly sloping limestone shelves, you will step across another little watercourse and not even notice that you have just crossed the headwaters of the River Ure, draining to the east. Even though somehow it felt as if you had already left Wensleydale by the time you had walked the first half mile of the Highway, it is now definitely behind you. Just over ¼ mile further, now no longer with any wall on your left but with the trees in Hellgill clearly showing ahead where it is and, with the stone parapet visible for quite a distance, you reach Hell Gill Bridge. As you cross it you also cross the infant River Eden, whose waters drain to the west; you have in fact crossed an important watershed. You are also leaving Yorkshire and the Yorkshire Dales National Park and entering Cumbria.

Hellgill is well named, for it is a remarkably deep chasm, a slash cut by water through the limestone strata. *See* photograph on following page. Erosion has carved the vertical walls into delicate flutings, bowls, fantastical shapes and the water now thunders through the bottom of the gorge in a series of cascades. Unfortunately, for a would-be spectator, there is so much vegetation, rowans in particular, that it is difficult to get a good view of Hellgill unless you either abseil into it with a rope or walk into it from its lower exit.

Reminder: Hell Gill Bridge is the point at which the main route and the high-level variation of this walk divide. Walkers on the main route go straight ahead; the high-level walkers turn left (west). The main route very shortly descends to the valley; the high-level variation descends slightly, but only as far as Aisgill Moor Cottages to cross the Settle–Carlisle railway. Thereafter, the route climbs to Swarth Fell and continues at a high level over Wild Boar Fell. If, when you reach Hell Gill Bridge, the weather has deteriorated so that there is little chance of good views on the high land, the lower-level main route will probably be of greater interest.

Before leaving Hellgill you may be interested to know a little more about Lady Anne Clifford since, even four hundred years after her birth, her influence is still felt and the evidence of it seen in these parts.

She was born at Skipton Castle in January 1590, the only surviving child of George Clifford, 3rd Earl of Cumberland and his wife Margaret Russell. The family moved to London where Anne was brought up around the Royal Court of Elizabeth I, her father becoming the queen's jousting champion. Unfortunately for Anne, when her father died when she was fifteen, he did not recognize her as his successor although, as her father's only direct descendant, she had every right to be. Instead, he willed his vast estates in Cumberland, Westmorland and Yorkshire to his brother, her uncle Sir Francis Clifford, with reversion to Anne only in default of male heirs. It was a decision that neither James I, after Elizabeth, nor either of her two husbands would do anything to overturn, but she never ceased to argue her case.

By her first husband, Richard Sackville, Earl of Dorset, she had five children, two daughters of which survived. Six years after his death she married Philip Herbert, Earl of Pembroke and Montgomery, and it was as Anne Pembroke, usually found as the initials AP, that she lived thereafter. Eventually she did in the end inherit the estate, when her cousin Henry died without heirs in 1643, as she was then the only legitimate successor. This was, however, in the middle of the Civil War and it was therefore not until 1649 that she came north again. She was sixty years old before she returned to Skipton Castle, which had been 'slighted' (severely damaged to prevent it being used as a fortress again) by Commonwealth troops during the Civil War, but Anne restored it almost to the remarkable condition in which it may be found today.

This was just the beginning of a vast programme of reconstruction and rehabilitation of many buildings all over her vast estates, always retaining the original style, and she travelled endlessly from one project to another for the next twenty-six years. Skipton Castle, Beamsley Hospital, Barden Tower, Brough Castle, Appleby Castle and Brougham Castle, as well as four or five churches, all benefited from her tireless efforts. Her journeys from south to north and back again frequently took her up Wharfedale and through Mallerstang, where she restored Pendragon Castle and Outhgill Church (*see* page 57). It was a journey undertaken at a time when roads were very rough and ready indeed, and it seems virtually certain that when she wrote 'I went over Cotter in my coach (where I think never did coach went before) and over Hellgill Bridge into Westm'ld', she traversed the route used by the drovers – and which you have used today. That is certainly why it is known as Lady Anne Clifford's Highway. Just imagine travelling that route in a coach! When you walk the Highway in the late evening, as I have done several times, it is not difficult to conjure up the ghosts of past travellers.

➤ Walkers who are taking the high-level variation via Wild Boar Fell, turn to page 65.

◄ *In Hell Gill*

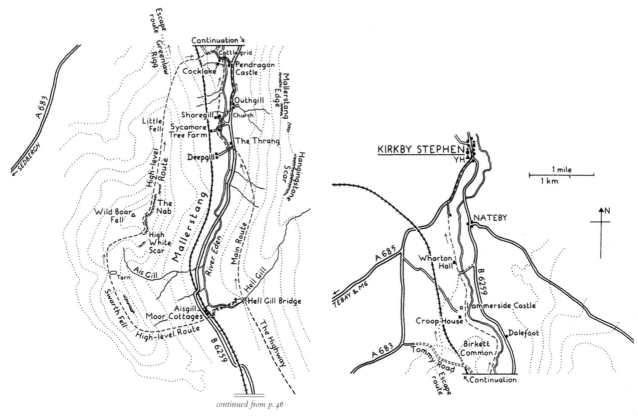

continued from p. 46

Hell Gill Bridge to The Thrang

Having crossed Hell Gill Bridge (closing the gate behind you, please), continue north, up a gentle incline and with a solid wall on the left once more. Whereas there was little sign of a track on the ground on the other side of the bridge, now there is a well-grooved one, except where it passes over exposed limestone pavement. Within a few minutes' walking, however, it again becomes a green way of velvety turf; appropriately, this bit of the Highway is called 'Hellgill Wold'. Slopes of rough sheep pasture rise gently to the right of the path; ravens croak in a landscape of wide skies. Then a line of nebs and crags, downfalls and screes comes into sight high above on the right, looking more impressive with every step. This is the series of rock scars collectively known as Mallerstang Edge although, according to the OS, that name only applies to that part of it which is directly above Outhgill.

Walking south to north it should be possible to distinguish Hangingstone Scar (recognisable by three stone men balancing on the edge), then High and Low Loven Scars, High and Low Band, Coalwell Scars (a name like that is suggestive, isn't it?) and Lindrigg Scars. As yet, none of the farmsteads in the Mallerstang valley, below

Hanging Lund waterfall ➤

and on the left, have been revealed, nor has the road, or the railway – although you know they must be there – for they are hidden below the lip of Hanging Lund Scar.

However, on the other side of the valley, it is impossible not to be aware of the massive Wild Boar Fell, its long escarpment defying the elements that have scoured and wrinkled its lower slopes. On a clear day you can pick out the stone men standing about halfway along the length of the highest stretch, on High White Scar. Perhaps some of them were there when the last wild boar in England was hunted on those remote slopes.

When you are approximately in line with the first of the steep crags above on the right, Hangingstone Scar, the wall turns sharply to the left and disappears out of sight down the slope below. The track continues ahead but now begins to slant downhill and, from walking on springy turf, the path traverses a rough fellside with ruts appearing in the track, holding puddles of water. Short-cropped green grass gives way to rushes; indeed, it seems a miracle that the few horses and sheep foraging here can find enough grass to sustain them. The path has descended below the limestone layers; no wonder the farmers sweetened their land with lime. Now scattered farmsteads appear below, each sheltered by a few trees. The railway can now be seen, and the road, the river, the walled fields. In Lady Anne Clifford's day there would have been few walls, if any.

The track fords one gill and shortly afterwards crosses another, still declining. It leads directly to a rusty gateway only yards from the B6259 and only 100 yds from the substantial building of The Thrang Country Hotel where, at the time of writing, a tea room is advertised as 'Always open for walkers and cyclists. Please ring bell.'

The Thrang to near Shoregill

Turn right along the road towards The Thrang, but only for about 25 yds before turning onto a gravel track on the left, where there is a public footpath sign for 'Deep Gill'. This track curves round to the right and crosses the River Eden by the little stone arch of Thrang Bridge, almost passing over what looks like another lime-kiln. On the far side of the bridge leave the track and turn sharp right along the river bank to a stone stile about 100 yds away. There is little sign of a path, but stay close to the bank – the river here is about 12 ft wide and fairly placid – and cross the pasture beyond, ignoring a farm bridge supported on a couple of girders. Follow the river round a bend to a gate. This leads immediately into a fenced farm track, across a little stream and so to a complex of farm buildings, but with no sign of a house. There is nothing to indicate ownership of the buildings but they must belong to Sycamore Tree Farm, which is just up the slope on the left, hidden by trees from here.

Reaching a metalled track on the far side of the complex, turn right through a gateway. From here, by looking across the walled fields more or less straight ahead, you will now be able to see, about ¼ mile away, the bell-tower of Outhgill Church, with several tall dark yew trees in the graveyard. The farm track leads ahead to a bridge across the Eden but before reaching it, take a faint trod to the left, marked by a finger-post, across pasture to a slit-stile. A faint path now continues along the left bank of the river, here heavily wooded with alders, as far as the bridge bringing the track to Shoregill (the buildings are just out of sight round a bend ahead) from the road down the valley.

From near Shoregill to Pendragon Castle

Here you have a choice to make: either cross the bridge and go to Pendragon Castle via Outhgill Church and the B6259, or continue into Shoregill and take field paths beyond the castle. Both routes are much the same length, and they are at the same level. In the rain, or when conditions are wet underfoot, the road route would be better because of firmer footing. The field path route is kinder to your feet and allows some good views of Pendragon Castle that you will not see from the road, but it is a little slower because of the need to negotiate more stiles.

To Pendragon Castle by Outhgill Church and the B6259

For this, cross the bridge to the right (east) bank and immediately turn left along it, so that the river is now on your left. A path across a little ditch, then through a gap in a wall ahead, leads across pasture to Outhgill Church. The river is only 50 yds away at a point where the waters rustle over shallows, a wonderfully soothing sound that must have helped worshippers and visitors over the centuries. In contrast, the metal kissing-gate into the churchyard was not designed for walkers with rucksacks on their backs and the spring on it is so fierce that only a determined effort (or holding your rucksack over your head) will enable you to squeeze yourself through without being caught like a rabbit in a trap.

Here we catch up with Lady Anne Clifford again. This church is The Chapel of St Mary in the parish of Kirkby Stephen and an engraved stone plaque on the outside wall of its entrance reads: 'This Chappel of Mallerstang after itt had layne ruinous

and decayed some 50 or 60 years was newe repayred by the Lady Anne Clifford Countesse Dowager of Pembroke, Dorsett & Montgomery in the year 1663 who all-soe endowed the same with lands which she purchased in Cawtley near Sedbergh to the yearly value of eleaven pounds for ever.'

It is a small and attractive building and appears to be in excellent repair, but I was unable to have a look at its interior as the front door is kept locked. This is a sad commentary on our own times. It used to be raiding parties from north of the border which were to be feared; now it is car-borne thieves and rustlers from the surrounding cities which force churches to lock their doors and farmers to combine in organisations like Farm Watch against them.

For the quickest route forward to Pendragon Castle via the B6259 simply turn left out of the church gate. You quickly pass through this little village of Outhgill (where there is a public phone box and some B&B accommodation) and as soon as the houses are left behind and a clear view is obtained ahead, the unmistakable ruins of Pendragon Castle are seen in a splendid position on a grassy mound, overshadowed by several tall ash trees. (*See* page 60 for details of Pendragon Castle.)

To Pendragon Castle via Shoregill and the field path

The gravel track into Shoregill leads past three buildings on the right, with a fourth on the left which, surprisingly, is a post office serving the several small communities in the valley. Immediately in front of this a sign (for 'Pendragon Castle and Kirkby Stephen') indicates the way through several gates close together, with a step-stile beside the last. This leads directly to a walled lane, although the left-hand wall is collapsed. At its end, go half-left to a step-stile (orange paint blobs) and another immediately beyond (more blobs) just to the left of a gate from where a track rises half-left up the slope beyond. Follow this track (more paint blobs on a stone and on a dead tree trunk) to an iron stile and then to an easy ford across the little drain of Moss Gill. There is a collapsing barn on the left, just across the gill, and from here you get a distant view of the ruins of Pendragon Castle.

The orange paint blobs now stop and a slight rise ahead interferes with the view, but a step-stile will be found in the wall ahead, about 30 yds from the right-hand corner. Immediately beyond this cross Riggs Gill and, bearing right, pass in front of another barn. Immediately beyond is a gate on the right, leading into another pasture bordering the River Eden again, and with an attractive view of the castle ahead. Shadow the river, crossing another little gill, until you approach the house at Cocklake, where a newish sign reading 'Goat-proof dog door' beside a stile shows

◄ Above *Outhgill church;* below *Wild Boar Fell seen from Outhgill churchyard* that you are definitely on the right route. Further signs lead you round the left edge of a paddock to a gate onto a tarmac road and a right turn here leads immediately to Castle Bridge, with the castle ruins well seen just a few yards along the road on the right. This road is Tommy Road, the fell road connecting Mallerstang to Ravenstonedale.

Pendragon Castle is surrounded by romantic legend, fact and fancy. The legend is that Uther Pendragon here raised the young boy who was to become King Arthur, he of the Knights of the Round Table, the warrior king of the Britons; this is presumably the source of its name. The fact is that the castle was built by Hugh de Morville, a Norman knight who was one of the conspirators in the murder of Thomas à Becket in Canterbury Cathedral in 1170. The building is unusual in that although it clearly had a moat surrounding the mound, it did not have a curtain wall, as castles had had for centuries, so it was quite possibly the model for other fortified houses and pele towers that were typical of this border country. As for the fancy, if you walk for no more than 50 yds or so down the road towards Kirkby Stephen, then turn round and look back at Wild Boar Fell, preferably in the afternoon so that the light turns its shape into a silhouette, the profiled face of a man can be clearly distinguished, as if lying on his back, with eyes gazing to heaven. It is reputed to be the face of Thomas à Becket, come to haunt Hugh de Morville for all time.

Lady Anne Clifford inherited Pendragon Castle with the rest of her estate and, great and determined conservationist that she clearly was, set about restoring it to its former grandeur, spending the Christmas of 1663 here with her family, the same year that she restored Outhgill Church. The Civil War was over by then and it is therefore not so easy to understand why, in the intervening period, it reverted to such a ruinous condition. Outhgill Church seems to be in excellent order and many houses built in Yorkshire about that time or before are as good as new, if not better. It can only be that nobody lived in the castle and so it was vandalized, masonry being removed and used elsewhere. Local people have told me that mullioned windows, as well as other architectural features from the castle, can be seen incorporated in a number of other buildings in the area. Once theft on that scale has begun weather begins to play its part and it does look now, from a distance, as if a couple of well-aimed cannon balls would bring what is left of it toppling down in a cloud of dust.

However, perhaps its future is now a little more optimistic. The present owner, Mr Raven Frankland, bought the castle in 1963 and, according to a newspaper report I saw, purchased it, in an extraordinary link with the past, *from the descendants of the original builders*. Mr Frankland and devoted helpers have been digging for over thirty years, removing tumbled masonry to reach the floor of the castle and finding ways into vaulted chambers virtually buried for years. Recently a grant of £180,000 by

The silhouette of Hugh de Morville on Wild Boar Fell

◄ *Pendragon Castle, the River Eden in front*

English Heritage has enabled much work to be done consolidating the crumbling walls and towers. By all accounts it has only just been in time.

Pendragon Castle to Lammerside Castle

Leaving Pendragon Castle, all walkers now being together, apart from anyone who took the high-level route traversing Wild Boar Fell but did *not* visit the castle (*see* page 70), should take the minor road (Tommy Road) which is signed 'Raven-stonedale 4'. (For those walkers who have walked the high-level route, this will involve retracing their steps for a short distance.) The road goes round a bend to cross the River Eden by Castle Bridge and continues up a slope to pass the house called 'Cocklake' on a sharp bend. Keep on for another 200 yds to where this hedged lane reaches a cattle-grid and then continues uphill over open unfenced fell.

Immediately beyond the cattle-grid bear to the right where there is a finger-post 'Public Bridleway Wharton' pointing north and follow an initially gravelly track which rapidly becomes another velvet-turfed green way. This curves gracefully

round the lower slopes of Birkett Common where the River Eden tumbles through a little gorge, Catagill Scar. Within a short distance, the track passes a lime-kiln on the left, which would provide good shelter in a downpour, as it is in excellent condition and has a rounded arch about 7ft high. It is built directly below several exposed small limestone scars, for Birkett Common is itself limestone.

The track trends downhill slightly to Birkett Bottom, passing a few isolated clints on the right and looking across the Eden to the little farm complex at Dalefoot. Here, although a green track does continue forward to a ford, bear sharp left (west) at a telegraph pole, and follow the track below the exposed and sharply upthrust limestone strata on Birkett Knott, seen above on the left. The way cuts across a bend of the river and then walks closely beside it again, bringing into view another picturesque ruin: this time it is Lammerside Castle and our route leads past it.

Go through a gate just below the farm of Croop House, which is on the left and not seen until you do, but then turn right immediately, through another gate. There is now little sign of the bridleway on the ground, but it passes directly in front of Lammerside Castle and its square-built crumbling tower. It has a sycamore tree sprouting out of the masonry on its north wall and its roots will undoubtedly see to it that more masonry will tumble before long. It certainly seems a pity.

Lammerside Castle to Kirkby Stephen

Go through a metal gate directly ahead and just right of the castle ruins, crossing a pasture beyond it and trending right to find another gate in the field corner, close to the river again. This leads across a fenced-off dry gill, leaving by a gate on its far side, then trend slightly left up the sloping pasture beyond. Reaching a gate at its top, the solid tower and buildings of Wharton Hall can be seen rising above trees ahead. Follow the fence on the right side of the next field, curving left at its far end, where it is bordered by a wooded gill containing Mire Close Bridge, to a gateway leading immediately onto a concrete farm track.

Turn right here and follow it straight ahead (north) and up a slight slope to the fortified house of Wharton Hall built, like Pendragon Castle and probably Lammerside Castle, in the twelfth century. (I should mention that my information might be wrong on this for Pevsner avers that no part of Wharton Hall is earlier than the fifteenth century.) The arrow-slits in the stout wall of what is now a barn, seen on the approach, leave little doubt as to the origins of this substantial structure. But it is interesting to see that Wharton Hall shows no sign of being at risk of crumbling into ruins like Pendragon Castle; the key to successful conservation is clearly the

◄ *Mallerstang seen from Birkett Common*

continuing use by people who care. Wharton Hall was successfully adapted to ordinary daily living throughout the centuries whereas Pendragon Castle and Lammerside Castle were not.

The concrete track leads straightforwardly through the complex of buildings and then continues, as a fenced carriageway between fields, to Halfpenny House, after which the concrete becomes tarmac. A short downhill slope leads to the A685 on a slight bend; it crosses a former railway line and leads directly into the outskirts of Kirkby Stephen.

Kirkby Stephen is a comfortable, friendly little market town in which to spend the night, with a busy tourist office that can help with a wide choice of accommodation and other information. Keep an eye open for the unusual sheep outside its entrance. There is no shortage of eating places and friendly pubs, both very welcome after today's exertions.

The Youth Hostel is in the centre, on the A685, in premises which were formerly a chapel, now sympathetically converted to retain pews, oak beams and stained glass windows. There are a number of interesting shops and it would be wise to check them out fairly closely for supplies either now or in the morning for there are no shops on the way to Keld, *or in it*, at the end of tomorrow's journey.

The imposing parish church of St Stephen is adjacent to the market place. It is built in a rich red sandstone and has a tall square tower; there is a splendid pillared entrance to the courtyard in front of the church which has a little bell-tower and a cross on its top. The inscription on it reads boldly: 'Built by the direction of the Will of John Waller Esq, a Purser in his Majesty's Navy and a native of this town. 1810.' What a fine memorial!

The entrance to the parish church of St Stephen, Kirkby Stephen

High-level variation: Hell Gill Bridge to Pendragon Castle via Swarth Fell and Wild Boar Fell

Note: This variation is about 4 miles/6.4km further than the main low-level route and has an extra altitude gain of about 1500 ft/457m.

Hell Gill Bridge is the point at which the high-level alternative to Pendragon Castle begins. Traversing Swarth Fell and Wild Boar Fell, it is a crossing of superbly wild terrain, high and exposed to bad weather but with magnificent views across the upper Eden valley. Assuming you are fit enough by now, the extra distance, compared with the valley route, should not seem significant. There are few obstacles, such as stiles, to slow you down and the actual route-finding, in good visibility, is very straightforward so you can really get cracking and cover the ground fast. There is, of course, the little matter of the height gain to consider but, unless you are carrying all the pots and pans plus the kitchen sink, that should not prove an insuperable problem.

Hell Gill Bridge to Aisgill Moor Cottages

Turning left through the gate on the north side of Hell Gill Bridge a good farm track leads slightly downhill to pass the buildings of Hellgill Farm, built at the point where the River Eden emerges from the ravine in a tumble of white water. As you walk down to a gate and then to another where the route crosses the river by a bridge, you have a good opportunity to pick out the line of ascent towards Swarth Fell on the other side of the depression ahead. In a couple of hundred paces the track curves sharply left away from the river, which now leaps over Hellgill Force immediately ahead. When in spate it can be quite spectacular, but you cannot really see it from the farm track unless you cross the ford just above it and then curve left a little behind a couple of ash trees on the rough ground.

Just past the gate at the entrance to the bridge over the Settle–Carlisle railway, you may notice a line of brick footings down the middle of the bridge. These were originally built because two farmers with land on both sides of the line became such bad enemies that they refused to speak or even to look at each other. There remained a risk that they might find themselves both crossing the bridge at the same time, so built a wall dividing the bridge into two; the footings still show where the wall stood. Sometimes people do unbelievably barmy things, don't they? Eventually either they or their successors decided, as always has to happen, that the only thing to do was to get talking, settle differences and pull the wall down.

As you reach the B6259 at Aisgill Moor Cottages, the highest point on this superbly scenic railway, you will realise that there is yet another inducement to tackle the high-level route, for here also is one of the friendliest little tea-rooms (and B&B) that I know anywhere north of Horton-in-Ribblesdale. Its situation here could hardly be better placed for a cuppa and some sustenance before tackling Swarth Fell, and Pauline and Bill will give you a real welcome.

Aisgill Moor Cottages to The Nab on Wild Boar Fell

Almost immediately opposite the railway bridge, look for a metal gate leading directly onto open fell. The finger-post here points out the bridleway to Grisedale, but you will find almost no indication on the ground that this is ever used. Anyway, the direction you need is not south but just south of west; uphill, not sideways. Initially there is not much to aim for, apart from the highest part of the high ground ahead; keep to the left of the shallow groove of Smithy Gill. The path, which roughly follows the county boundary, frequently seems to disappear in the coarse moorland grass tussocks and occasional boggy patches, but you may be able to pick out a single large and isolated boulder about halfway up the slope to act as a marker. It has almost certainly stood here since the retreat of the last Ice Age, ten thousand years ago, when Wild Boar Fell and nearby Baugh Fell were under the centre of the ice cap.

A steady plod and a last pull up the final slope leads to a couple of cairns about 20 yds apart on Swarth Fell Pike. Nearby, a gritstone edge outcrops just below the highest land, enhancing wide panoramic views across the Mallerstang valley. Stroll along this to its northern end, where there are more cairns, including a particularly spiky one in a rash of stones. To the north, across the wide depression or combe drained by Ais Gill, the sharp escarpment on Wild Boar Fell is now clearly seen and is the next objective.

The actual highest point on Swarth Fell is at the northern end, a spot height of 2234 ft/681m, and from here a well-marked path runs northwards, following the line of the broad ridge linking Swarth Fell to Wild Boar Fell, curving down to a depression which holds an unnamed stagnant tarn. Beyond the depression a path continues up the other slope to the north, then curves rightwards (NNE) on the plateau of Wild Boar Fell. *Do not go that way*: it will lead you to the summit trig and a large stone wind-break but you will miss all the best views, for it crosses the top of the plateau instead of following round the escarpment. Instead, after leaving the tarn,

Above Wild Boar Fell seen from Aisgill; below Mallerstang seen from the path to Swarth Fell ➤

watch for another path which veers much more noticeably rightwards, to the north-east, curving round The Band, the northern slope of the combe of Ais Gill. This leads just a little higher than the escarpment of Low White Scar and onto the fine edge of High White Scar, looking out over Mallerstang. There are four or five tall cairns here, visible over great distances. There is also a spot height here of 2322 ft/708m, which is exactly the same as that given for the official top.

The edge of the escarpment is now an infallible guide. It is scenically much more interesting than the flat plateau and its craggy rim is more deeply incut than the map suggests. Following the faint trod round for ½ mile you reach The Nab, a jutting outcrop of bare gritstone rock. Here the stones have been piled together in a flattened mound, a tumulus, probably the grave of an Iron Age chieftain. There is also a single cairn.

The Nab to Tommy Road and Pendragon Castle

A fairly steep but short descent off The Nab now follows, with the shattered crags of Scriddles falling away on the right. An obvious path has been worn along the edge of

the escarpment but it soon becomes more of a grass trod as the angle eases and, about ten minutes after leaving The Nab, it flattens out as it reaches an area where there is a small outcrop of limestone clints, an intrusion into the prevailing gritstone at this altitude. Some of these have been fashioned into a horseshoe-shaped windbreak, with a cairn nearby.

Just a few minutes beyond this windbreak (about ¼ mile) and still losing altitude, the path along the edge reaches a wall corner, where a large area of land has been enclosed on the Ravenstonedale (left-hand) side of the ridge.

Looking directly across Mallerstang from here, to the slopes on the far side of the valley, you can pick out the line of the Highway, used by the main route, slanting across the fell and reaching the road in the valley bottom at The Thrang. Nearer to hand, a glance half-backwards down the right-hand slope will show where an old green track, a bridleway, rises from Mallerstang, beside a series of limestone pavements. I understand that this is the route of a proposed trail supposedly suitable for horse riders, some sort of alternative Pennine Way. If it ever happens, unless stone slabs are laid to create a causeway, you will no doubt find the ground here, and down the slopes on both sides of the ridge, churned into mud, creating unsightly scars. I have nothing against horses; I'm just against the damage their hooves could do on ground like this.

The path now continues beside a wall on the left and along a grassy and almost level balcony as far as a sudden short dip, beyond which it starts to rise again. On the far side of this dip the wall turns sharply away to the left, so our path is now once more climbing open land towards the rounded hump of Little Fell. Just before the top of the rise there is a whole family of cairns, Mum and Dad, three teenagers and a titch, all lined up to admire the view over the valley below; the single cairn on the highest point is just 70 yds further on.

A fairly obvious grassy track, with occasional ruts, turns down the slope beyond, continuing north, but after about 600 yds a wall reinforced by a wire fence appears on the right, where a large area of land has been enclosed on the Mallerstang slope. When the angle shortly steepens a little, the track forks and the main branch, the one to the left, continues ahead. *Do not follow this track* – unless you are short of time and need to take the shortest possible route. In that case, *see* page 70.

Instead, follow the right-hand trod which, although less defined, stays close to the wall on the right. It curves gently away (to the right) from the main track and then passes in between the wall and a deep swallow-hole (Moor Pot) on the left which takes all the drainage here and whose bottom is full of rushes. It shortly passes a second but smaller hole then, still close to the wall on the right, turns sharply downhill to the east, towards Mallerstang. The trod becomes very faint in the rough

◄ *One of the 'stone men' on High White Scar, looking north*

pasture but the wall, which now has a gill on its other side, remains a sure guide down the slope towards the tree-fringed railway line. On this short descent you will also be able to spot the tarmac of Tommy Road just beyond the bridge crossing the Settle–Carlisle railway, which here first crosses an embankment and then immediately enters a cutting. The bridge is between these and is soon reached by slanting slightly left down the pasture. Once crossed, the unfenced tarmac is reached on a bend about 200 yds away.

Turn right along Tommy Road – the unfenced fell road connecting Mallerstang and Ravenstonedale – and in a further 300 yds you reach a cattle-grid. Although the route forward to Kirkby Stephen turns left at this cattle-grid, you will have seen on the descent from Little Fell that the romantic ruins of Pendragon Castle in its splendid situation beside the River Eden are now very close at hand. Just cross the cattle-grid and simply follow the walled lane slightly downhill and round the bend. As soon as you have crossed Castle Bridge you will see the ruins over the wall on the right.

See page 60 for the description of Pendragon Castle and the forward route into Kirkby Stephen.

Variation on the high-level route omitting Pendragon Castle

Note: The variation is a short cut which will save about 1¼ miles/2km on the day's overall distance. If, through lack of time, inclination or even by mistake, you do not follow the wall down the fellside towards Pendragon Castle as suggested above, continue along the track (the main one, keeping left (north) when it forks after leaving Little Fell) along the broad grassy ridge of Greenlaw Rigg. You will reach Tommy Road, but ¾ mile further west than the main route. Just before you reach the tarmac, ensure that you have a small walled enclosure, with a barn next to the wall, on your immediate right. On reaching the unfenced road, go straight across it and back onto open pasture and you will almost immediately see a walled green lane with two barns on its left-hand side.

Follow this for ½ mile, soon with the Settle–Carlisle railway line alongside on the right, and cross the line by a bridge. Turn left (north) on the far side of the bridge and follow the track for 300 yds to the junction with a tarmac road. Turn right here and then immediately left down another track towards Low House, turning left again (north) in front of it. A concrete track now leads forward and in about ½ mile reaches a point where the main route joins from the right, near Mire Close Bridge (*see* page 63). From here you continue straight ahead, to pass Wharton Hall and complete the last short leg into Kirkby Stephen.

Day Four

Kirkby Stephen to Keld

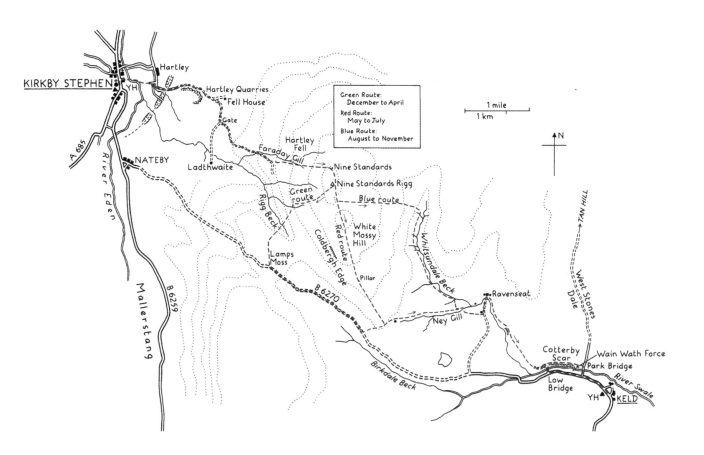

- ➤ *Distance:* About 10½ miles/16.8km (The Green route – see text – is about 2 miles/3.2km longer)
- ➤ *Altitude gained:* About 1650 ft/503m
- ➤ *Terrain:* After about two miles of firm tarmac, the crossing of the high land via the Nine Standards is over peaty ground, which can be rather boggy in places; then good paths complete the stage from Ravenseat into Keld.
- ➤ *Refreshments:* none; stock up in Kirkby Stephen.

In travelling from Kirkby Stephen to Keld, you are re-crossing the main Pennine watershed (first crossed on Lady Anne Clifford's Highway) and re-entering Yorkshire. Whichever way you go, it must be over the high gritstone moorland, for there is no low-level alternative to this stage – unless you count tramping over the unfenced fell road, the B6270, which links Nateby, a mile south of Kirkby Stephen, to Keld as a lower-level version. (At its highest point the road is at 1700 ft/518m above sea level, whereas the highest point of the cross-country route, the trig point at Nine Standards Rigg, is not much higher at 2172 ft/662m.)

On a day of driving rain and mist, when the cross-country routes may seem profoundly unappealing, simply following the road may seem to be a good option. You will not lose it, that is for sure. You do not have to walk on the tarmac because there is a grass verge for almost the whole way; there is almost no human habitation after leaving Nateby and there is very little traffic. You may even cadge a lift (as if you would!). Or (and I hesitate to even breathe this option, although I confess to having used it myself in bad weather) ring Kirkby Stephen 71741 and get Mr Thompson's taxi service to convey you to the outskirts of Keld in style. Assuming you do set off up the road and then the weather clears so that you can see where you are going, there is a good and quite well-signed path from the highest point of the road, via Lamps Moss, to enable you to rejoin the cross-country routes at Nine Standards Rigg. In brief, poor weather is not necessarily a disaster and for some walkers, including your author, it can provide a navigational challenge heightening the eventual sense of achievement. When it is too easy you do not appreciate it.

Let us, however, for once assume the best – a day of scudding clouds and bright sunshine, with shafts of light illuminating the surrounding fells; a day when skylarks are singing their hearts out, your legs are strong and you are at ease with the world. On such a day, the crossing over England's central watershed back into Yorkshire is a delight. Alfred Wainwright's Coast to Coast Walk, which crosses the same high land has, however, become so popular in recent years that erosion by booted feet on this crossing of the peaty high ground has caused some concern. From my experience, that erosion is simply not in the same league as that on the Yorkshire Three Peaks Walk, or on sections of the Pennine Way, but it is undoubtedly happening. This has led to attempts to 'manage' the problem and the current solution, which at the moment seems eminently sensible and should command the support of all environmentally aware walkers, is to designate different routes for different times of the year so that the ground is given the opportunity to recover in its 'close season'. I will explain this more fully shortly, and since these different routes do not diverge until you have covered about 4½ miles anyway, there is no immediate urgency.

Frank's Bridge over the River Eden, Kirkby Stephen ➤

Kirkby Stephen to Nine Standards Rigg

Leave Kirkby Stephen from the market place in the centre of the town, right next to the church of St Stephen. Look for a sign reading 'To Frank's Bridge and the River Eden'; from here a walled lane winds a twisting passage gently downhill to reach them both. Alternatively, between a branch of Barclays Bank and the 'Devonshire' bakery and confectionery shop (a useful place to obtain a few supplies for the journey ahead), a narrow ginnel sneaks between high walls, bearing left at the end, to reach Frank's Bridge by a slightly different route. Next to it is a building named 'Brewery House', hinting at its original use.

At the time of writing (March 1996) there is a sign, erected by the Yorkshire Dales National Park Authority, just before you cross the bridge, which is directly relevant to today's walk and requires your attention. It explains that 'continual use of just one route will lead inevitably to a badly eroded peat quagmire and the need to lay a stone path. Either would reduce people's enjoyment of the walk [the Coast to Coast Walk is assumed to be the route in question] because they would be less com-

fortable to use than a natural path and would create ugly scars across the fell.' There is only one public right-of-way but this arrangement allows for two other (much more convenient) permissive paths across the high land. A map attached to the notice shows these three routes, coloured in green, red and blue, and apportions periods of time when each should be used: *see* page 76. These objectives seem to make good sense in principle and I therefore urge walkers to cooperate in making the scheme work.

As you cross the bridge on a clear day, today's major objective, the tall stone columns or cairns of the Nine Standards, can be seen on the distant skyline to the south-east. Turn right after the bridge and follow a good path along the north bank of the river until it bends away. The path continues to the east, beyond a kissing-gate, as a narrow tarmac strip at the left edge of a field, rising gently to meet a walled lane at another gate. In 150 yds a T-junction with a minor lane is reached in the pleasant village of Hartley and here you turn to the right; in a further 100 yds a path marked by a yellow arrow turns off to the left to cross Hartley Beck by a footbridge and to join the road on the far side. Here you turn right again and follow the road uphill,

past the old railway viaduct and the entrance to Hartley Quarry which, continuing uphill, you follow left around its northern edge. The workings are extensive, with deep excavations and many warning signs of the dangers, but from the quarry's top rim you can again see, to the ESE, the stone men of the Nine Standards beyond intervening fellside.

The isolated buildings of Fell House are in the little dip just ahead and then, beyond a cattle-grid and gate, the tarmac comes to an end where the road forks. You have gained about 650 ft/198m of altitude over the two miles to here and have about 1000 ft/305m to gain on the two miles that follow, so the angle is going to steepen a little.

Ignoring the track to the right, signed to Ladthwaite, the one to the left, signed 'Public Bridleway Rollinson Haggs', is gated immediately ahead with a sign reading 'Coast to Coast path'. In a further 200 yds or so, there is another gate and sign: 'Coast to Coast Walk and Nine Standards. Due to severe ground damage the path has been re-routed. Please follow the waymarked permissive path.' The track leads ahead obviously, soon with a wall alongside on the right, enclosing the valley of Rigg Beck, and passing a collapsing barn. From the top of the rise here there is another view of the Nine Standards, ahead and now much nearer. Beyond the barn, both wall and track shortly cross the bed of a stream, so that the gill is now on the left; then in a further 200 yds, the wall turns further right (south-east). On this corner there are more signposts, one showing the new map with the red, blue and green routes (as displayed at Frank's Bridge) and another pointing just south of east which reads 'Permissive path Coast to Coast Walk and direct route to Nine Standards'. (It is at this point, incidentally, that Wainwright's Coast to Coast Walk has been re-directed.)

This path is the one needed, a stony track which soon becomes grassier, climbing beside the grooves and deep-cut ravines of Faraday Gill, on the left, towards a small but well-made pointed cairn ahead. From this cairn two more can be seen ahead, on each side of the gill, and beyond these is yet another, higher up. The track has dwindled to a path up this slope, a path reinforced with small gritstone slabs over the now peaty ground. (I cannot say that I find these offensive.) Then there is one final well-made cairn before a short but sharper pull leads directly to the Nine Standards.

If you are lucky, you will be able to enjoy a wide and extensive view from here, to the Howgills in the west and over the Stainmore Gap to the north towards the Scottish Borders. The Standards themselves are some of the biggest cairns to be found anywhere in the north of England: the smallest is about 8 ft high, the biggest is more like 10 ft and with a considerable girth. Collectively they have a considerable

◄ *The fell road from Hartley leading to the Nine Standards*

'presence', enhanced by the mystery as to why they are there at all, for there is no certain explanation. If you are unlucky, the great shapes will loom out of swirling mist, making you feel as if you are in the company of a small army of giant wraiths.

From here, a bearing just east of south (170 degrees grid, 175 magnetic) leads slightly uphill in 150 paces to reach a view indicator erected by the Kirkby Stephen Fell Search Team, then a further 300 paces or so on the same bearing leads to the trig point on Nine Standards Rigg.

Three Seasonal Routes from Nine Standards Rigg to Ney Gill

These three routes are designated and marked on the management map shown at Frank's Bridge as being 1) the Green route, operative from December to April; 2) the Red route, operative from May to July; 3) the Blue route, operative from August to November. The Red and Blue routes are virtually the same length (3 miles/4.8km), while the Green route is 5 miles/8km long. All routes converge at Ney Gill, leading forward into Ravenseat and thence by a common route (with a slight variation possible) to Keld. (This last section is also the same as the Coast to Coast Walk as, apart from the road, it is the only route worth considering.)

The Green route to Ney Gill (*December–April*)

From here, the faint, but cairned path of the Green route heads south-west to reach the B6270 road at its highest point. This path is the one that has been used for about twenty years (in the opposite direction) by the participants in the 23-mile charity walk or run known as 'The Mallerstang Horse Shoe and Nine Standards Yomp'. Head south-west from the OS column on a path which is faint on the stony ground but which becomes more obvious once peaty ground is reached. It is marked by occasional cairns, soon crosses the stream of Rollinson Gill and then crosses Rigg Beck, just outside the intake wall. From here it shortly swings south to traverse the limestone area of Lamps Moss and reach the B6270. Turn left (SE) here and follow the road for just over 1½ miles until you spot a Land Rover track turning to the left (east). This goes as far as a shooting-hut (where the Red route joins) and then the public footpath continues down Ney Gill to a finger-post just outside Ravenseat, where it is joined by the Blue route. (The finger-post reads 'C to C' and points west up Ney Gill with a green arrow, and east towards Ravenseat with a white arrow.)

The stone beacon on Coldbergh Edge, on the Red route ➤

The Red route to Ney Gill (*May–July*)

From the OS column on Nine Standards Rigg just east of south (170 degrees grid), past a small collapsed stone shelter and a cairn and then slightly downhill to reach two finger-posts, one of each side of a wide, peaty grough. From the finger-post on the far side of the grough (and ignoring the line of marker-posts heading east, which indicate the Blue route effective August–November via Whitsundale and described next), continue slightly uphill on the same bearing as before, just east of south, 170 degrees grid, to cross the slightly higher ground of White Mossy Hill. Virtually due south from here you should now be able to see a prominent stone beacon; when reached (it is about a mile away) it will be found to be a beautifully constructed pillar on the edge of the sloping plateau and commanding fine views, especially to the west and north. The path from it continues to the SSE for a further ¾ mile to where it intersects with a Land Rover track onto which you turn left (east) to pass a shooting-hut in about 300 yds where the Green route joins. (However, if you turn right along it, it will soon bring you to the B6270 road and more quickly to Keld if required.)

The Blue route to Ney Gill via Whitsundale (*August–November*)

From the OS column on Nine Standards Rigg head just east of south (170 degrees grid) past a small collapsed stone shelter and a cairn, close together, and then go gently downhill to reach a wide and peaty grough which has finger-posts on each side of it (this is identical to the Red route so far). On the far finger-post is a 'C to C' sign pointing 95 degrees grid, i.e. virtually due east (a sharp turn to the left), and from here a row of yellow-topped marker posts indicate the route towards Ravenseat via Whitsundale. The posts lead for several yards across an almost level peaty gritstone moor, with only a few grouse to notice your passing by, then trend gently downhill, crossing a few groughs en route and arriving at another 'C to C' finger-post just before reaching the beck in Whitsundale. Here you change direction, turning south, the path keeping generally well above the loops and curves of the beck and along its right (west) bank. Several small sheepfolds in various stages of repair are passed, one having a little corrugated-iron shelter attached to it. Eventually, about ¼ mile before reaching the first of three barns which can be seen in line ahead, the path crosses a wire fence by a ladder-stile and heads towards the barns until stopped by an intake wall. Here a finger-post indicates a sharp change of direction to the right (south).

Walking slightly uphill, with the wall now on your left, you reach the top of a rise in 100 yds where there is another finger-post, a stile over a fence and the remains of what was once a small barn. From the evidence of its end walls, which are all that are now standing, it was originally roofed with an arc of corrugated-iron sheets which have now rusted away. (Older readers will recognise the shape of a large Nissen hut.) Immediately down the far slope is the shallow beck of Ney Gill, and a finger-post saying 'C to C' and pointing west up Ney Gill with a green arrow, while a white arrow points in the easterly direction towards Ravenseat, just downstream. This point marks the junction of all three routes: green, red and blue. From here into Keld is common to all three.

Ney Gill to Keld

The three routes having now joined up, the mutual way forward is by a narrow path that picks a way between the beck on the right and the wall on the left towards Ravenseat, reaching a transverse wall with a blocked-up stile. Here a finger-post says 'FP Keld 3' pointing you across the stones and then up beside the wall on the far

Low Bridge just before Keld, with Cotterby Scar above ➤

side, then curving back left to regain the easterly direction, the intake wall being kept on your left. The path is obvious enough and leads quickly to a junction with the unfenced tarmac strip into Ravenseat at a gate and cattle-grid.

Here you turn left and into the hamlet, crossing first a stone hump-backed bridge and then a wood-plank one, heading towards the cottages opposite. Before reaching them, yellow paint dots indicate the path shadowing Whitsundale Beck on its left (east) bank. Beyond a second gate, a finger-post directs you up a grassy slope to a barn, then to pass a disused farmhouse and another barn and all the while tracing a route above the left-hand side of a fairly deep and wooded gorge. This has several pleasant cascades: a little way along, Oven Mouth, part of the high and steep bank, collapsed into the foaming beck far below at some time in the past, leaving a rocky precipice exposed. The OS map shows the paths forking here but keep to the right fork and to the right side of a small enclosure. Then a stretch of open fellside leads to another finger-post ('Ravenseat' ¾, Keld 1¾') from where the B6270 comes into sight below at the point where a road bridge crosses the infant River Swale.

The path now slopes down to an apparently abandoned farmhouse where the remains of two cannibalised Land Rovers were rotting away quietly when I passed, and the cart track from here continues downhill in the direction of Low Bridge.

Just before the last, steeper, part of this descent, a yellow arrow points to a higher path along the top of Cotterby Scar and it is a nice choice whether to take it or not. If you do not, but descend and cross Low Bridge and then turn left to walk along the road into Keld, you will get fine views of the attractive limestone cliffs of Cotterby Scar which provide such an attractive backdrop to the waterfall of Wain Wath Force. If you continue along the higher-level path, you will avoid some tarmac but will not have the views of the cliffs or quite such good views of the Force. You will also have two tall ladder-stiles to climb before your path joins the Tan Hill road on a steep

Keld, with the Swale gorge behind

◄ *Looking up Stonesdale near Keld*

bend just north of Park Bridge, where you turn right, cross the Swale, then turn left along the B6270 to complete the long ¼-mile walk into Keld.

On the whole, for once I think the tarmac and the better view is the preferable way. The delightful Swale scenery here will provide the perfect complement to the wildness of the moors now left behind.

Keld is only a tiny village, essentially a little collection of houses and chapels, built on a little loop road off the B6270, in a splendid situation at the head of the Swale gorge. Apparently there used to be a pub, but the building was purchased in order to turn it into a chapel. It is, however, significant as the junction of the Pennine Way and the Coast to Coast Walk and the Youth Hostel here (found on the right-hand side of the B6270, 100 yds after the first turn off into Keld) must be one of the most strategically-situated ones in the country, especially as the choice of alternative accommodation is limited, as mentioned in the Introduction.

A sight well worth seeing on a fine evening, however, is Kisdon Force where the River Swale tumbles over some rocky sills (there is an upper and lower force) in its deep gorge. It is fairly soon reached by anticipating the first part of tomorrow's walk, and a round trip of about three-quarters of an hour would give ample time to appreciate it. The details are given on page 86.

Day Five

Keld to Reeth

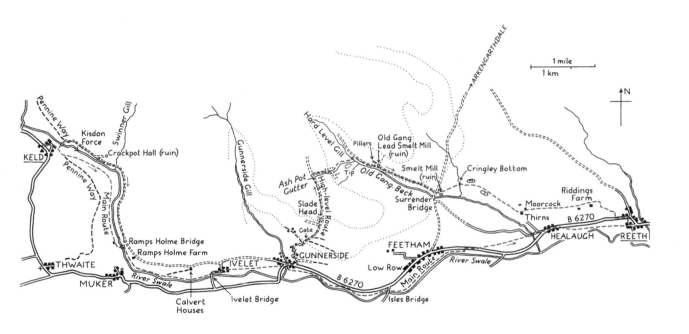

- ➤ *Distance:* About 11¾ miles/18.8km on main route; about 12¾ miles/ 20.4km on high-level variation
- ➤ *Altitude gained:* Negligible on main route (about 1000 ft/305m high-level variation)
- ➤ *Terrain:* Good paths throughout the main route (and almost entirely so on the high-level variation).
- ➤ *Refreshments:* In Muker (if you divert slightly) or in Gunnerside where there is a choice (both routes).

There are a couple of variations to today's section of the walk. Before leaving Keld you will need to decide on which side of the river you are going to be for the first couple of miles; then from Gunnerside to Reeth there is a high-level variation to enable the walker to get some idea of the fascinating history of lead-mining in Swaledale and to see something of its industrial relics.

There can be no doubt at all but that the loveliness of Swaledale is in its valley, not in the ravaged moors above it, where the lead-miners toiled. This particularly applies to the superb Swale gorge as far as Ramps Holme Bridge, so that is the way the main route goes. However, the choice as to whether to go by the west bank or the east is a nice one, for the rival attractions are finely balanced. I personally prefer the west bank (although only marginally) and so that is described as the main route, but readers must make their own judgement.

Briefly, on the one hand, if you use the west bank you will be walking mostly on a good footpath, occasionally stony but often grassy, and will have the opportunity to divert slightly to view Kisdon Force, the biggest and best of the Swale's waterfalls. This is also the least-used route – which must be a major plus. On the other hand, if you choose to go by the east bank, you will be able to view East Gill Force (which, however pretty, is only a sideshow compared to Kisdon Force). You will also pass close by the ruined Crackpot Hall (and with a name like that you may find it irresistible – I know I once did) which is in a splendid situation for views down the Swale gorge. The drawback is that almost all the walking on this east-bank route is on a wider, harder surfaced (but not tarmac) bridleway. You cannot do both on the same day so, if you have not decided earlier, you have got just 300 yds after leaving Keld in which to make up your mind. *See* page 87 for the east-bank route.

As you leave this delightful little village, shod in your modern boots and water-proofs in your pack, spare a thought for a former cleric of Keld, the Reverend Stillman. In 1789, the year of the French Revolution, requiring money for the repair of his church fabric, this tough gentleman walked all the way to London and back, asking for donations as he passed on his way. He was heard sympathetically and returned successfully, with all the necessary funds in his pocket. It also says a great deal for the charitable hospitality with which he must have been helped along his way, for his total expenses for the double journey were only sixpence! Nowadays there is no church, but two chapels.

Leave Keld by the walled lane south-east and signposted for Muker. In about 300 yds it forks, with both branches signposted for the Pennine Way. You may well notice here, and not for the only time, that the post also carries discreet advertisements for accommodation, for Keld is, of course, a staging post on both the Pennine

Way and the Coast to Coast Walk. This fork is the point at which the die is cast: turn left and you will be opting for the east bank, to be described shortly.

Keld to Ramps Holme Bridge via the west bank

Keep straight on south-east, and in about 100 yds the track passes through a gate. In a further 150 yds there is a finger-post pointing to the left, signed 'FP Kisdon Upper Force' where a narrow path turns downhill. Even though you may wish to see Kisdon Force, ignore this sign and keep on the main path for another 200 yds or so as it passes below a limestone scar (on the right) and then reaches a large cairn. Here the tracks diverge, with the Pennine Way continuing on the right fork as a path rising to the south-east. (There is normally a 'Pennine Way' finger-post here, but when I last passed by it was lying on the ground.) Taking the left fork, our route briefly climbs to the top of a little rise directly ahead, with a clear view down the valley of the Swale, and from here on the path leads gently downhill towards the valley bottom.

Kisdon Force in the Swale gorge

On its descent it shortly passes a stone gateway from where a less-used path slants down back left, enabling a visit to be made to view the several waterfalls of Kisdon Force

If you decide to visit the waterfalls (which will only add 15 minutes or so to your day), take care when reaching the bank if the slabs there are wet. I have never heard of anyone losing their footing here on damp (and then invariably slippery) limestone and tumbling into the flood, but you don't want to be the first. The upper cascade is perhaps 8 ft high, but the lower one falls over four lips, the lowest giving the biggest drop. They are a fine sight, particularly after heavy rain when the thunderous roar is magnified in the confines of the vertical walls of the gorge. Return to the main track by the same route.

I should say that this way of seeing the falls is currently safer than the alternative, the one indicated by the finger-post mentioned above ('FP Kisdon Upper Force') because although it seems easy enough to begin with, once it has passed below a large limestone buttress, sections of this path have collapsed, leaving a loose and muddy slope directly above the river that some walkers may find intimidating.

At a point roughly opposite the place where Swinner Gill, on the other side of the valley, joins the Swale, there is an area with the curious name of Hartlakes. From the discovery of pigs of lead stamped with recognisable markings, it is known that the Romans were engaged in lead-mining in Swaledale almost two thousand years ago. What is much more astonishing, at least to me, is that according to a book I have read Hartlakes has been identified as the possible site of a foundry used by, of all people, Egyptian metallurgists, working here seven thousand years ago. The mind boggles; but the Egyptians did build all those pyramids, didn't they? They must have terrified the Ancient Brits.

For a short way this path follows an ancient lane with collapsing walls, then winds downhill over short-cropped sward until it is a green ribbon threading a way between occasional barns and walls along the almost level valley floor. This path passes through the edge of a little alder wood close to the river, then more lovely turf leads towards Ramps Holme Bridge, which can be seen spanning the river a little way ahead. Reaching a stone barn, the path forks; the right branch leads into Muker (which is certainly worth visiting if you set off early enough and have time to spare) but the left branch is marked with yellow arrows to the left of the barn and then along the bank of the Swale, at a section where some parts have had to be shored up to prevent further collapse.

Ramps Holme Bridge is single-person width only, but is supported on stone pillars; the width of its span, however, gives some indication of just how much water can flood down here after really heavy rain. I suppose that if it ever does get washed away, there is only ever likely to be one person on it — if that is any consolation.

Having crossed the bridge, turn right at a finger-post signed for Gunnerside. The alternative route down the east bank of the Swale joins here (see below), with both routes continuing down the valley together.

Alternative route to Ramps Holme Bridge via the east bank

Having left Keld by the walled lane heading south-east and signed for Muker, on reaching the junction signed for the Pennine Way in both directions, take the *left* turn. This leads down a wooded sunken lane to a gate, bearing left once through it to a footbridge across the River Swale. The Pennine Way and the Coast to Coast Walk briefly cover the same ground here and there are finger-posts for both as the path slants up a field beyond the footbridge, shortly passing close by the attractive little East Gill Force which can be seen in a wooded dell on the right. At the top of the field the path joins a good track and here our route (which is here also coincident with the Coast to Coast for a short way) turns right (east), the track passing immediately above East Gill Force and through a gate just past it. This level cart track curves round a bend, passes a point where another (private) track slants steeply down to the right, towards the gorge, and continues along the top of West Wood.

Here you are above the deepest part of the Swale gorge. At one point, an old land-slip has carried away some of the slope below and the trees with it, enabling you to have a view down to the foaming river at the bottom of the gorge, which would be otherwise unseen. Even so, although it is possible to pick out the deep pool into which Kisdon Force empties, the cascades themselves cannot be seen from here. Above, on the left, are the old Beldi Hill lead-mine workings, whose grey spoil-tips were visible from Keld.

The track makes a left-hand bend (where an old miners' footpath leads up into the combe above), passes a barn on the right and then, in another 150 yds or so, it forks. The main track now continues ahead, slanting down towards the valley floor, and is the way our alternative route takes. To visit Crackpot Hall, however, take the less-used left fork, which quickly leads directly to it. (The Coast to Coast Walk goes this way, turning uphill onto the moors.)

Crackpot Hall was once a well-built farmhouse; now it is in a very tumbledown state, with collapsed roofs and walls falling down, having been finally abandoned in about 1950. Rabbits run around everywhere, as cheeky as schoolkids who know they can't be slapped nowadays, and the slope in front of the house is a wilderness of nettles. It would be a depressing place to visit but for its view, which is unquestionably a fine one, looking out over the wooded slopes of the lower part of the Swale gorge to where the river flows through a mosaic of walled fields.

Crackpot Hall's pitiful condition now is the result of subsidence caused by lead-mining, mainly during the nineteenth century, but it also has some history attached to it. It was at the centre of a very bitter dispute (about 1760) between the two rival mining enterprises of Parkes and Company (who mined Beldi Hill and some of whose spoil-heaps can be seen directly behind Crackpot Hall), and the Wharton Estate (who mined veins reached from nearby Swinnergill). The row was all about mineral rights and mining concessions and, so far as I have been able to sort out the truth from the confusion, was because Parkes and Company sub-let a mining con-

cession (on the edge of Crackpot Hall land) to two partners, Metcalfe and Scott. This led to miners from Lord Pomfret's Wharton Estate flooding some of their opponents' workings, and driving them out of other workings by violence. There was a smelt mill at Oxnop in those days (further down the valley) and Pomfret's men seized the ore there, claiming that it had been extracted from workings on land on which only Lord Pomfret could grant leases. It all led to Lord Pomfret losing his legal case, being fined £400 and being committed to the Tower of London for non-payment. That sounds very medieval, doesn't it? Now the dust and clamour of those battles have long settled and there is just the bleat of a sheep, the croak of a raven, or the 'G'back! G'back!'of a grouse to interrupt the distant noise of running water.

Leaving Crackpot Hall to the rabbits, the main track heading for the valley floor is quickly regained (just turn down the slope to the south-west for 100 yds) and gives a fast descent on a mostly firm and stony track. Where it crosses the end of Swinner Gill, there are a few more ruined mine buildings but then it is straightforward level walking along an obvious cart track which fords the several little gills draining the slopes below Arn Gill Scar and Ivelet Boards. About 400 yds before reaching Ramps Holme Farm and opposite – although slightly above – Ramps Holme Bridge, watch for where the footpath crosses the bridge, turn off the main farm track and join this footpath on the right. The east bank and west bank routes have now joined, on the east bank.

Ramps Holme Bridge to Gunnerside

The delightful walk that now follows is almost entirely on the level, tracking the north bank of the River Swale. In about 100 yds the path forks, the left-hand one towards the farm buildings, but take the one trending to the right, signed 'Gunnerside via Ivelet'. This proves to be a trod across beautiful buttercup meadows sprinkled with barns; there has been nothing like this since you walked the meadows between Askrigg and Sedbusk in Wensleydale. The path almost touches the river just south of the farm, then cuts across the bend ahead. It is worth looking back from time to time along here for some lovely retrospective views to the hill of Kisdon and the gorge. The path then runs close to the river again for a short way before again forking. This time the left fork makes for Calvert Houses, but keep right, signed for Ivelet Bridge.

This right-hand path keeps close to the bank of the Swale, here lined with alders and pitted with rabbit warrens, then easy walking across more meadows leads to the

◄ *The Swale gorge seen from near Crackpot Hall*

high-arched Ivelet Bridge, almost hidden by trees and clearly built in days before motor cars, for it is only wide enough to take one car, and if that has a long wheel-base you will surely scratch its bottom.

At Ivelet Bridge, leave the river by a wicket-gate at its side and continue left uphill on the narrow tarmac road, heading east and shadowing the river until, after a couple of hundred yards, it curves uphill to the left and into the hamlet of Ivelet. This is so tiny that you will hardly have time to take more than a couple of breaths before you are out of it again, almost immediately turning right in front of the public phone box, passing Ivelet Farm House and Salt Pie Cottage, to where a narrow path (finger-post) leads down to a footbridge across a wooded beck. Slit-stiles show the way across the sloping meadows ahead, now traversing some distance away from the river. After crossing a few pastures, the path climbs up to the little bank of Marble Scar, from where you find that you are looking down on the patchwork of walled fields of Gunnerside Bottoms. The path again forks here, the right fork sticking close to the river and heading for Gunnerside Bridge, but keep on the left branch, at the higher

Looking towards Gunnerside from Ivelet

Looking back west over Gunnerside ➤

level. More slit-stiles lead to Gunnerside village, entering it on a signed path beside some cottage gardens and emerging very close to the Post Office. This also sells ice-creams and other goodies, the pub (the King's Head Inn) is only a cock-stride away and there is plenty of accommodation for any walker who is seeking it. It is a good place to pause.

Gunnerside was an important centre for the lead-mining industry, which brought great prosperity to Swaledale, but by about 1890 it was faltering to its end as the world price of lead dropped and the veins of ore either ran out or proved uneconomical to mine. Some of the evidence of the tremendous activity of that era still exists and can be seen in Gunnerside Gill and in Hard Level Gill. There is little of beauty in these industrial remains, but plenty to arouse interest so, in addition to the valley route continuing from Gunnerside to Reeth, I have also described a higher-level variation which climbs over the moor between Gunnerside and Hard Level Gill, enabling a walker with some time in hand to see something of it while there is opportunity: *see* page 97.

Gunnerside to near Feetham

Locating the King's Head Inn, which is just east of the bridge over Gunnerside Gill, in the centre of the village, the public toilets will be found just down its right-hand side (as you look at it from the front). These are useful not only for their normal purpose (wasn't it the great Duke of Wellington who remarked that 'the wise man has a pee when he has the opportunity and only a fool waits until he has to'?), but because the footpath heading down the valley and crossing Gunnerside Bottoms starts at a slit-stile immediately next to them. This flat and fertile area is scattered with traditional stone barns and divided up by a network of dry-stone walls. Apart from the gateways used by farm machinery, there is an obvious line of slit-stiles leading across the pastures, shadowing the road. The path uses these to the far side where it rises up a short slope to a gate and joins the road, but only briefly, for it immediately turns off it on the right and slopes down to the river.

The path is now signposted along the right-hand edge of a hay-meadow, on the river bank and staying close to it until the road and river are so close together that there is no room for a footpath at all and you must walk on the tarmac for about 200 yds. The path begins again at a metal gate on the right, a grassy track leading to a slit-stile, then passing in front of an attractive house with a stand of trees and trending towards the river again, which here has extensive pebble banks. Still following the bank of the river across more level meadows, it keeps left when the river encloses an island of pebble banks and curves round to reach Isles Bridge, where there are steps leading up to a slit-stile on the edge of the road using it. (The OS map shows the footpath crossing this pebble island, but you would nowadays probably have to wade to use it.)

A left turn along the road for 30 yds leads to another stile on the right (and a sign 'FP Reeth 3½'). Here it is best to climb easily onto the broad flat top of the wall bordering the river and walk along its top because, although there may well have been a footpath on the ground on its right side at some time, it is now totally choked with vegetation. When the wall ends the path continues along the top of a grass-topped embankment, with the brown waters of the Swale sometimes 10 to 12 feet below on the right and the meadows 3 or 4 feet below on the left. The straggling villages of Low Row and Feetham are both by-passed and the fine green turf becomes more of an earthy path as it goes through a belt of mixed woodland. Rather suddenly you reach a finger-post signed 'Reeth' and the path slants sharply back left and up a bank through the woodland to reach the B6270 road again (at another finger-post reading 'Isles Bridge' pointing back the way you have just come).

◄ *Gunnerside Bottoms:* above *Looking west to Gunnerside;* below *Looking east from Gunnerside*

From near Feetham to Reeth

Here you are just about ¼ mile east of Feetham, which is home to the popular Punch Bowl Inn – if thoughts of a convivial halt should chance to cross your mind. If you do turn back to the Punch Bowl, retrace your steps to the finger-post afterwards for the next short stretch of the road needs your close attention if you are not to miss the path. About 300 yds after reaching the road at the 'Isles Bridge' finger-post, watch for a grassy drive on the left, half-hidden by vegetation and slanting towards a house named 'Robin Gate' (the name is also incorporated in the metal gate on the roadside 50 yds further on). Immediately past the house, go up a couple of steps to a wicket-gate on the left of the road, where there is a finger-post signed 'FP Healaugh', and a grassy path then leads eastwards, shadowing the road below on the right, across sloping pasture to a slit-stile beside a gate. It continues in the same line, via two metal gates (currently with a dead elm tree beside the second) then descends slightly towards a barn, passing through a gateway and a slit-stile just before reaching it.

There are pretty views to Scabba Wath Bridge (where the minor road from Grinton to Askrigg crosses the Swale) and also to the 'bottoms' outside Healaugh as you

walk along here. A belt of woodland appears ahead, across the line of march. A faint trod leads past the barn to a slit-stile, on the far side of which is a metalled road (Healaugh to Surrender Bridge, via Kearton). Turn right down the tarmac slope and in 50 yds the road crosses Barney Beck, at Barney Beck High Bridge, here flowing rapidly down a wooded gill. Stay with the road, bypassing on the left the tree-lined drive leading uphill to Thiernswood Hall, to reach the B6270 again. Here turn left into Healaugh (sign 'Reeth 1½m').

Healaugh is a pleasant little village with nothing to offer any temptation to a walker to linger apart from a phone box until, at its far end, just beyond the last building on the right (Manor House Farm), there is a green space with a couple of bench-seats. There are also two finger-posts, one for 'Reeth and Grinton via river side' (which is the longer way) and one simply signed 'Reeth', which traverses the fields above the river and is more direct. Taking this latter way, the route shadows the road, via a slit-stile and gate, past a large piece of tree trunk polished by sheep rubbing against it, to a slit-stile at the side of a barn and above a marshy area. Descending slightly, it continues past the wooded head of an old landslip above a bend in the river and, after a couple more slit-stiles, trends away from the river again. On the last ¼-mile into Reeth, keep just left of a wall which funnels you into a walled lane. Passing the children's playground and then the doctor's surgery on the left, take

Looking up Swaledale, from just outside Reeth

◄ *Approaching Healaugh from Feetham with Scabba Wath Bridge crossing the River Swale* either of two footpaths, both signed, which lead between houses to the main road in Reeth, turning right along it into the centre.

Reeth is clearly an accommodating place for tourists and walkers, with plenty of friendly pub/hotels, bed-and-breakfast establishments, shops and other temptations to linger a while. Many of these are built in a large square around the sloping green crossed by the main road, giving an opportunity to stock up with any supplies that may be needed for the morrow, especially for walkers not staying overnight close to the centre of Reeth. Reeth gives the impression of an open and friendly place, an impression soon confirmed. Its days as a lead-mining centre have been gone for a century and it certainly seems to have managed the transition to the present successfully.

You may notice that, unusually for a place of this size, Reeth has no church; this deficiency is supplied by the beautiful building at Grinton just a mile away on the other side of the Swale. Walkers who plan to stay at the Grinton Lodge Youth Hostel (on the hillside above Grinton) have a particularly good opportunity to visit this, 'the cathedral of Swaledale', for they pass it just before they begin the last uphill trudge to their night's lodging.

High-level variation: Gunnerside to Reeth via Surrender Bridge

Note: This variation is about 1 mile/1.6km further than the main low-level route and has an extra altitude gain of about 1000 ft/305m.

This variation is intended for walkers who, having walked the valley route from Keld as far as Gunnerside, might then prefer a change for the second half of the journey, especially since the opportunity to see some of the industrial relics of Swaledale's lead-mining past will be lost once you have walked east of Reeth. The route therefore climbs out of Gunnerside roughly to the north-east, crosses the heather moorland to reach Hard Level Gill and then Surrender Bridge, then continues to Reeth using a high-level track. (The last part of the way is the same route as that used by Wainwright's Coast to Coast Walk.) It provides an unrivalled opportunity to have your cake and eat it, to savour the delightful and intimate river scenery of the Swale gorge and the valley bottom as far as Gunnerside, then to climb high above it, while still maintaining progress down the valley.

The OS map shows a network of right-of-way footpaths and bridleways on the moors above and to the north of Gunnerside, the routes that were used by the lead-miners going to and from their work. But that was a century ago. Nowadays, apart from some re-working of some of the spoil, the only product, if that is the right word, of these moors is grouse. On the moorland between Gunnerside and Hard Level Gill some of the paths shown on the map can therefore only be traced with difficulty on the ground and in the meantime new tracks have appeared to facilitate access for the sportsmen with their guns. It is therefore in everybody's interest, sportsmen and walker alike, to use these newer tracks where they have superseded the old ones, for the grouse will be disturbed less and fewer walkers will run the risk of having pellets in their backsides. The route I have recommended across this section (Gunnerside to Hard Level Gill) is therefore, I believe, the best one possible and gives the fastest walking over what would otherwise be very tiring terrain.

Gunnerside to Surrender Bridge

Walk east towards Reeth from the centre of Gunnerside along the B6270 and after about 200 yds turn left uphill on a tarmac track or drive, signed as a cul-de-sac and

◄ *The imposing square at Reeth*

sometimes with a gate across at the bottom. This climbs sharply and in about 50 yds the tarmac strip makes a sharp left-hand bend; follow this round to the left, ignoring the unmade walled track that keeps heading east towards Staney Gill Quarry and Heights. The tarmac strip (which is both footpath and road serving several houses and converted barns higher up) continues to rise to the north and is an infallible guide onto the moor.

It gives a steep climb but gains height quickly, overlooking the houses of Gunnerside below on the left. You may notice that one of the highest of the converted barns, on the left, has half a dozen letter-boxes on posts, each box with a name for the owners of a group of three or four even higher properties (probably those at Potting) not attainable by Postman Pat's delivery van.

It is not easy to reconcile the OS map with the tarmac road, but it is certain on the ground that the zigzags end as the angle eases. The tarmac then looks as though it is heading for the buildings at Potting, but a ravine intervenes and the strip turns right (east) to skirt its edge, on the left, allowing a grand view over the defile of Gunner-

side Gill. Just ahead, the tarmac ends at a gate through an intake wall, just above a half-derelict barn near to which is a finger-post for a footpath for Low Row, pointing south-east. (For anyone wishing to be certain where they are on the OS map, at this point you are at grid ref 956987 immediately south of spot height 405m and next to the blue letters 'Spr'.) Beyond the gate, grassy tracks diverge, but the objective now is a junction of paths at the grouse butts on Slade Head. So take a grassy track to the right, climbing to the north-east. When it forks in 100 yds keep left, still north-east, up onto open moor where rabbits skip around like fleas in the grassy areas amidst the encroaching heather. At the 490-metre contour (about 1600 ft) the track forks again, with a solitary stone in the middle of the grassy triangle between them, and here you take the right fork, heading north. A rutted track of gravel and grass now leads forward and within about 150 yds you will start to pass a line of stone grouse butts, which continues for about 300 yds. Here you are on Slade Head and the last butt is on the top of the moor; 50 yds beyond it is a flat area for parking and turning vehicles.

The ruins of the Old Gang Lead Smelt Mill

◄ *Gunnerside Gill from the track towards Slade Head*

From here you can look over to the right (north-east) down a long heather slope leading to Hard Level Gill and you can see tracks in its bed. What you cannot yet see is any obvious way to reach them, despite the right-of-way paths on the OS map.

Keep on along the only obvious track here, heading north (the continuation of the one by which you reached the butts) and it shortly crosses the little stream of Ash Pot Gutter by a ford. Immediately past the ford turn right (east) and follow another good gravel track down the left bank of Ash Pot Gutter, ignoring a track re-crossing the beck on the right and the calls of the grouse telling you, 'G'back, G'back!' Grouse butts shortly appear on the left of the track you are on and ahead, on the far side of Hard Level Gill, you can see what looks at this distance like a line of tilted gravestones on the bank above the bed of the gill. Rather disconcertingly, the gravel track ends abruptly just before reaching the last butt. However, a good track can be seen only 150 yds away at a lower level and there are only a few patches of heather and some limestone outcrops to cross, reaching it next to a large spoil-tip (spot height 1463 ft/446m). A gated embankment crossing Hard Level Gill is just ahead and a right turn on its far side leads directly to the main track heading south-east where the Coast to Coast route is joined.

The little cascade of Hard Level Gill is close by on the right and not easily seen, but of much more interest now are the curious objects up on the bank to the left. A short scramble to them shows that what had looked like gravestones from a distance are two rows of stone pillars, about fifty in total, each about 6 ft to 8 ft tall and square but for the fact that their outer faces are tapered like flying buttresses. There are walls at each end of the rows and partially collapsed intermediate walls make it clear enough that this was once a long roofed building; in fact, it was the peat store used to fuel the Old Gang Lead Smelt Mill, whose ruins are just below. This grouping of roofless buildings and piles of stone in an area of spoil-tips and levelled ground beside the beck is dominated by a tall chimney. The building attached to this was where the galena, the lead ore, was roasted before smelting. A closer look among the debris behind this chimney reveals the arches of the flues of the four smelting furnaces which fused into one great flue running up the fellside behind the ruins. It is almost totally collapsed now, but it did the essential job of carrying away the highly toxic fumes from the process. The whole site is now a scheduled ancient monument and much good work has been done in consolidating the remaining stonework; responsible visitors will not clamber on the walls or do any damage.

The firm gravel track down the gill soon reaches Surrender Bridge where a tarmac road crosses from Feetham to Arkengarthdale.

Ruins of the Surrender Bridge Smelt Mill ➤

Surrender Bridge to Reeth

Cross this road, going east, about 30 yds north of the bridge, at a 'Footpath' finger-post, keeping to the higher track when it forks ahead and immediately passing above the ruins of the Surrender Bridge Smelt Mill. The remains of the flue from the two ore-hearths can be fairly easily distinguished, climbing the hillside to the north.

A reasonable path now leads forward to the ENE, whiteish stones marking the way between occasional wet or boggy patches, and passing a cairn on a mound ahead. From here you find that you are looking across the ravine of Cringley Bottom, and the path leads to its rim. The descent into it is steep, at an angle of about 45°, but the path is straightforward and unless it is muddy you are unlikely to heed Alfred Wainwright's comment that the best descent is accomplished on your bottom. A good selection of stones enables a dryshod crossing of the lively beck and then pocket-steps climb the far bank to a gated slit-stile.

From here a pleasant grass track leads due east, with a solid intake wall on the right for the first 500 yds; when the wall ends the track leads forward but now veering right, towards the south-east, passing an enclosure with an isolated barn away on the left (Cleasby) and gradually becoming stonier underfoot. In about 500 yds after leaving the wall end, keep to the higher of two paths in order to pass to the left (north) of a two-field isolated enclosure. The path now becomes more of a cart track, funnelling downhill between walls, by-passing an isolated cottage in another

field enclosure on the left, and leading directly to the farm at Thirns. A metalled track continues downhill to Healaugh from here, but our route turns left and uphill now, on a concreted slope, to pass directly in front of the isolated cottage named 'Moorcock'.

From here a good earth and gravel track continues to the east, slanting upwards briefly where it passes through a zone of old spoil-tips. It then contours just above the intake and enclosure walls on the right. When this track, after the point where there is a sharp right turn into the property of Riddings (being refurbished when I last passed by), becomes little more than a green trod sloping down towards Riddings Farm on your right, leave it for a well-used footpath that trends leftwards at a slightly higher level (still going east) across some open moor towards a cairn. Just beyond the cairn, rounding a wall-corner on the right, you reach a gate at the entrance to the walled Skelgate Lane.

Skelgate Lane is narrow, quite sunken in places, and fairly overgrown with brambles, blackthorn and other sorts of vegetation that catch at your clothing as you pass down it. However, the narrow stone path down its middle is clear enough to get by these obstructions and, with one sharp turn to the right as the houses of Reeth come into view below, it leads quickly to the main road. A left turn here leads downhill to the square and the comforts of civilisation. From here on, lead-mining and the stern moors are left behind as you rejoin the main route to Richmond on the final day. Now is an opportunity to stock up on any necessary supplies for tomorrow, especially for walkers not staying overnight close to the centre of Keld.

Looking east over Cringley Bottom towards Reeth

Day Six

Reeth to Richmond

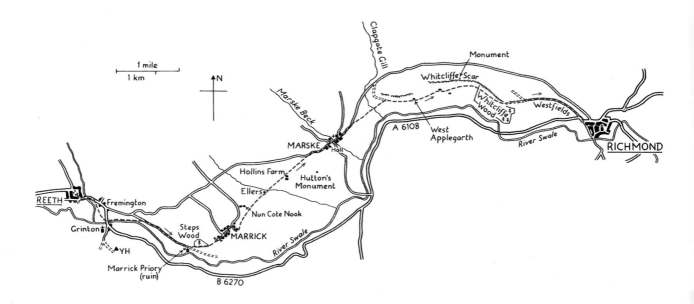

- ➤ *Distance:* About 10½ miles/16.8km
- ➤ *Altitude gained:* About 750 ft/229m
- ➤ *Terrain:* Mostly on good paths and tracks, but the route is very faint across some pastures, requiring careful route-finding.
- ➤ *Refreshments:* None; stock up in Reeth.

For this final stage, after walking beside the Swale for about a mile, the route rises above the valley to undulate across two intervening low ridges before traversing a wide shelf just below the line of scars that fringe the Swale valley just west of Richmond. The wild moors have been left behind and the landscape has many fine woodlands, especially near the end of the walk, giving a day's walking of great interest and some sections of great beauty.

It would be possible to walk more closely by the side of the river by using

St Andrew's Church and Grinton Bridge from the road to Marrick Priory ➤

footpaths or tracks from Marrick to Downholme Bridge, but from there you would either have to climb back uphill to Marske, or have a dreary tramp along the A6108. The public footpaths employed for this stage therefore are almost, but not entirely, the same as those used by Alfred Wainwright in his Coast to Coast Walk, for he chose the best, indeed almost the only logical ones. This does, however, have the advantage that at certain places 'Coast to Coast' signs and yellow markers help greatly with navigation. There is one complicated bit at Marrick, so the route description is particularly detailed there.

Reeth to Marrick

If you spent the night in Reeth, the day's walking begins by heading east out of town to cross Arkle Beck at Reeth Bridge. About 200 yds after crossing this, look for an obvious footpath leaving the road on the right, initially beside Arkle Beck, but then trending away from it on a well-used trod across level pastures to reach Grinton Bridge over the Swale at a slit-stile. Walkers who stayed overnight in Reeth should now take a golden opportunity to cross the bridge and visit the lovely Grinton church, the finest in Swaledale. If you spent the night at Grinton Lodge Youth

Hostel, you have a second chance. On the north side of the bridge a finger-post indicates where a good footpath now continues eastwards along the north bank of the Swale. This path is contained by a new fence on the left and is fairly well trodden, with several stiles at cross walls. At its end it rises slightly away from the river to join a metalled track, which has just branched off the Reeth–Marske road, where you turn to the right.

Looking across the Swale from here, Grinton Lodge (originally a shooting lodge) is an imposing sight on the hillside opposite, backed by a stand of trees, and there is a charming retrospective view to Grinton Bridge and its ancient church. But as you

tread the tarmac, which often has circular bales of straw piled three high on its verges, you will catch glimpses ahead of a tall square tower; this must quicken your interest for it can only be Marrick Priory. Getting nearer to it brings some disappointment, for what is clearly an ancient tower sticks up out of a rash of modern buildings, mostly belonging to Marrick Abbey Farm. There are Nissen huts, corrugated-roofed buildings, silage towers, old water tanks, rusty and galvanised metal of all kinds, black plastic silage clamps with old tyres piled on top, rusty machinery of all kinds: what a tip! As you walk past, a sign advises that some of the buildings are used as an Outdoor Education Centre, supported by English Heritage. Signs discourage any other than authorised parking. The few ruins of the Priory visible from the roadside, apart from the tower, seem to be a large Gothic window embrasure and part of an adjacent wall. Marrick Priory, established some time in the twelfth century, was inhabited by a few Benedictine nuns but, like the nearby Cistercian Ellerton Abbey on the

Marrick Priory, from the gate entering Steps Wood

The River Swale and the approach to Marrick Priory

other bank of the Swale (of which only a single solitary tower still stands), it was dissolved under the orders of Henry VIII.

Just beyond the Priory, on the left, is a gate and footpath sign 'Marrick ¾' and a pleasant grass path slants from here to a gate at the entrance to Steps Wood. Looking back from here, there is at last a view of Marrick Priory that conceals those parts of the scene which turn it into a rural slum, and which reveals something of the beauty that still lingers. The path rises through the edge of the wood on old stone flags next to a wall, with wooded slopes rising to the left.

The path is almost a sunken one, which is as well for three or four trees have fallen across the route and it is necessary to duck under them. Reaching a stile at the exit from the wood, a glance over the wall on the right reveals a brief view of the Swale down below: it will be the last for some time. With the wall still close beside you, the now grassy path reaches a gate beside a barn, with a small gated enclosure on its other side. A double finger-post here may raise doubts, but take the left-hand direction which is the continuation of the path you are already on. It leads alongside the wall to another gate at the entry to the straggling village of Marrick

Marrick to Marske Bridge

A converted Wesleyan Chapel (1878) is on the immediate left and a little further along the metalled lane, but on the right is a small building which its ecclesiastical-style windows suggest was once a church although it looked to me as if it has been converted

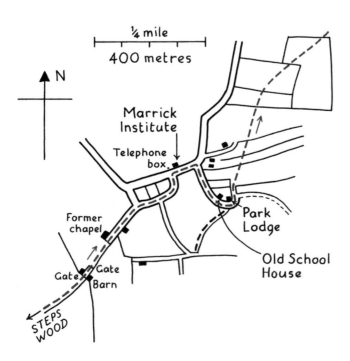

to a dwelling. On the left, a house with a plaque declaring that it was the old blacksmith's shop is passed, then the road bends left (north) and reaches a T-junction, with a public phone box almost opposite. Turn right here, pass the Village Institute and look out for the 'quaint sundial' that AW noted on the Coast to Coast Walk: it is a wand sticking out of the wall of the last cottage on the left, with an arc of Roman numerals below it to mark the time.

The road now forks, the left-hand way being the main road; the one you need is that to the right (south-east), comforted by a finger-post reading 'C to C' pointing that way. This lane bends left, passes 'The Old School House' and then, next to it, a house named 'Park Lodge', where the tarmac ends. A 'Coast to Coast' finger-post points north from the corner of this last house, into a lane which, however, in less than 50 yds turns rightwards into a field, where it peters out. Instead of turning into the field, go straight ahead (NNE) to a slit-stile directly ahead and then, following yellow arrows, via more stiles set close together and dodging over some land graced, if that is the term, by some tatty old railway goods waggons used as animal shelters and a large 'modern' barn (which means that it will not last long compared with the 'old' ones). The path is now visible across more fields, rising gently onto higher land and you now have a much wider vista of surrounding hills.

A tall obelisk is visible on one of these hills to the ENE and is roughly on the line of march ahead, although to its right and at a higher elevation, as the path now descends towards the valley of Ellers Beck to the north-east. The path ahead is not at all clear on the ground but is just to the left of the line to the tall obelisk seen ahead on one of these hills to the ENE. It descends towards the valley of Ellers Beck, on a convex slope which makes it difficult to spot one stile from another, but you quickly reach and cross the farm track to Nun Cote Nook and then signposts point the way, still north-east, down two large fields to reach the renovated and isolated house of Ellers, which has no access road to it. Perhaps its owner walks everywhere, or uses a helicopter?

It may be worth mention-ing as a cautionary tale that, on my own last visit, these last two large fields contained cows, suckler calves and a bull. On my own I can be quite brave because cattle do not usually take much notice of a solitary person. But I had my dog Henry with me. He does not, with good reason, like cows (or worse, bullocks) and the feeling is mutual; they always do their best to bump him off, so he tries to stay near me. The path slants right

Ellers

across these fields and the nearest gate is as far away as possible. I immediately put Henry on the lead, and set off to cross the first field but realised that the cattle in the next had spotted us, then felt distinctly wimpish as I tried to sneak along the edge of the second field as fast as I could go, while the cattle started to move towards us *en masse*.

With a sigh of relief I reached the slit-stile turning into the paddock bordering Ellers Beck and thought I was safe. But as soon as I had crossed it, I realised that my way to the footbridge, beside the house on its right side, was blocked by what looked like a very large bull indeed. I was on the right-of-way path, but I have my doubts whether that would have impressed the bull. I didn't want to put his possible friend-liness to the test, and I scanned the field-edge for an escape route. It looked as if I could reach the right-of-way path on the other side of the stream by ducking between the strands of the wire fence beside the beck then wading the beck rather than crossing the footbridge, so I grabbed Henry, tucked him under my arm and made a dash for it. I then found that access to the correct path was blocked by a thick hedge reinforced with barbed wire, and had no choice but to wade downstream and somehow clamber onto the footbridge to get back onto the correct route. I might as well have faced the bull. This is the sort of hazard that walkers with dogs have to learn to deal with, for farmers must be allowed to graze their cattle on fields crossed by footpaths.

From the plank footbridge the way slants uphill north-east to a gate in a field cor-ner (no cattle in these, thank goodness) and then in the same direction towards the top left of a stand of trees sheltering Hollins Farm, reaching the farm track at a gate. The path on the ground now disappears, but the right-of-way is clearly shown on the OS map as going north-east, that is half-right across the track and up the sloping pasture ahead. A low wire fence traverses this, across the line of march, but if you look to the right along the track you may spot a gate which will enable you to divert a little to avoid the inelegant manoeuvre of climbing the wire, although posts and the lack of barbs on the wire indicate where the crossing point is. Then slant rightwards up the next field to continue alongside its bounding wall. You reach a stile in a cor-ner, with a nearby finger-post, turn through a gate in the wall on the right and then go over a slight rise and north-eastwards down the field beyond to reach the road into Marske just opposite a cottage, at Hardstiles Top. Here you turn right, downhill towards Marske Bridge.

The tall obelisk, Hutton's Monument, that you saw earlier from near Marrick is now on the wooded heights above you on the right; it is certainly on a fine view-point and was erected in the grounds of Marske Hall in memory of Captain Matthew Hutton in 1814. The Huttons of Marske Hall, the entrance to which is passed almost at the bottom of the hill as you near Marske Bridge, were a famous family in these parts, but the number of sons named Matthew causes some confusion. One Matthew Hutton was apparently Archbishop of Canterbury in the seventeenth century and yet another Matthew Hutton was Archbishop of York. A Hutton with a quirky sense of humour was the Sir Timothy Hutton who, according to an old book by one J. S. Fletcher (long out of print), arranged that when an entry was being made in the Richmond parish register concerning the birth of a bastard daughter to two local citizens, the place of birth was given as a certain orchard in the town. Marske Hall itself is nowadays evidently converted into flats, but you see nothing of it as you descend the hill towards this village built, and almost hidden, in a wooded hollow. You will, however, certainly appreciate the fine trees and the beauty of the scar-fringed subsidiary valley of Marske Beck as you look across the slopes on your left.

Marske Bridge to Whitcliffe Wood

The OS map Outdoor Leisure 30, Yorkshire Dales Northern & Central areas, unfortunately does not cover the final part of this section, the last stretch into Richmond. It does, however, show the way as far as East Applegarth and the entry into Whitcliffe Wood and from there onwards the way is so obvious that use of a map is hardly necessary at all.

There is a junction of roads at Marske Bridge, but go straight ahead (which is in fact half-left) up the hill beyond: the road sign reads 'Whashton and Ravensworth' and there is also a 'Coast to Coast' sign. Passing the lovely twelfth-century church of St Edmund on the left, turn right at the T-junction and, still going uphill, leave the village behind. You are now looking for a footpath crossing fields on the right of the road and any temptation you might feel to pass through any field gates before you reach this path is discouraged by notices reading firmly 'No Access'. You find that the path is not at a gate but at a stile, on the second bend after the T-junction and at a point where the road starts to go downhill slightly. If you are lucky, there will be a finger-post reading 'Richmond 4½ miles' but, when I saw it, it had been snapped off and was just balanced on the wall (and after the cold winter of 1996 I would not be surprised if it had been nicked for firewood). The line of the path is, however, fairly clear and it heads across a wide dip towards the wooded limestone flanks of Applegarth Scar facing you. There are five stiles of the step-over or squeeze-through variety at the intervening walls or fences, then, always heading for the right-hand end of the scar, you cross the wooded Clapgate Beck by a concrete footbridge. An obvious path now climbs to the NE towards a telegraph pole, then between fenced pastures and up towards a large white-washed cairn. When reached, this is found to be on a level cart-track on a shelf below Applegarth Scar and leading to West Applegarth Farm.

From this track there are delightful views down to the lovely Swale valley below and the numerous dark yews beneath the scar add variety to the woodland colours. It is only a pity that the caravans on the Swaleview Site are so obvious; they all seem to be painted to stand out like sore thumbs.

The track leads past the front of the buildings of West Applegarth Farm but peters out just beyond it. However, about 100 yds ahead is a stone barn, with a faint yellow arrow on it pointing to the right through a gate next to it. Once through the gate you turn sharp left in front of the barn to see a slit-stile ahead, marking the way. (Some wag has put a sign here, beside the barn, reading 'Coast A Del Sol' and when you look back you find that on the other side it reads 'Coast A Brava'.) Yellow dots on visible places on succeeding stiles now lead you to contour across the slopes to

reach a tarmac track (to Low Applegarth, now renovated and seen just below). Now either turn left and follow this track (or use a stile to cut the corner across the intervening field) which immediately curves round to the right and passes the renovated barn at High Applegarth. The track continues to the last of the Applegarths (East), which is a working farm and advertises a 'camping barn'. Instead of going through the farm, the path leaves the track at a stile on the left and then yellow arrows and footpath signs point forward to join a most attractive and delightful green way contouring below the wooded Whitcliffe Scar, rising steeply on the left, and eventually leading into Whitcliffe Wood.

As you walk along, glance up to the skyline on the left to see a small fenced-off obelisk, the memorial to Willance's Leap – although it must be said immediately that the leap was made by Willance's horse. It is not a vertical drop, but the ground below the spot is certainly very steep and, not surprisingly, it was the last leap that the horse ever made.

Apparently Robert Willance, a local squire from Richmond, was out with a

Approaching Whitcliffe Wood

◄ *Low Applegarth and the River Swale beyond*

hunting party in 1606 (although my book by J. S. Fletcher says it was 1696) when his horse bolted over the edge of the scar. The horse was killed, but Willance himself survived unscathed and in gratitude and thanks to God presented a silver chalice to the town of Richmond, which is still preserved today. Stories of leaps over chasms or down precipices are not uncommon in Yorkshire and I can immediately bring to mind the story of Robin Proctor's Scar on the edge of the plateau of Norber, in the limestone area near Austwick, where a horse ridden by a farmer of that name made an almost identical leap to Willance's horse. Dick Turpin was supposed to have urged Black Bess to leap across Hell's Gill when pursued by the Sheriff of Westmorland's men, as mentioned earlier. I am sure there are others, but I cannot recall details.

Whitcliffe Wood to Richmond

This lovely track leads into Whitcliffe Wood at a gate and then continues to rise gently through it. At various points you may well spot containers like oil-drums set back from the path; these contain grain to feed pheasants and there are certainly many of them here, squawking furiously as they fly off with a clatter of wings at your approach.

Leaving the wood, with gorse on the hillside on the left, the now gravelly track passes by the buildings of High Leases Farm, on the right, and then a distant but pleasing view of red-tiled roofs and the dark-beige tower of Richmond Castle can be seen half-right ahead. Beyond Richmond a level plain stretches into the grey-blue distance. The track becomes tarmac just beyond High Leases and a minor road undulates for a way before beginning a long descent down the pleasant suburban road of Westfields.

It is worth mentioning that you can leave the tarmac on this descent for a parallel path across

Richmond seen from the south

open grass slopes on the right, and there are several bench seats on which to take a rest and admire a grand view over this part of the Swale valley. Where Westfields joins the main Reeth road, on the corner of Quakers Lane on the left, you may notice an interesting plaque on the wall above. Erected by the Automobile Association it reads: 'Solar Eclipse   June 1927   Centre Line of Totality'. Proof positive that the sun does not always shine even on Yorkshire.

Entry into Richmond, especially on foot, is undoubtedly something of an event

Evening light on Richmond Castle

for a first-time visitor. From the end of Westfields cross Reeth Road into Cravengate and then take the first left down Newbiggin to see an elegant street elegantly pre-served. At its end, look across the cobbles to the right and down Bargate, descending steeply towards the river. It is a view that has been essentially unchanged for cen-turies. If you continue bearing slightly left out of Newbiggin and then sharp right down the narrow Finkle Street, you emerge into the remarkable cobbled Market Place. Rising up directly ahead of you, in the centre of the market place and surrounded by shops and inns, is the ancient church of Holy Trinity, with a great tower opposite also overlooking the square. Next to the church is the obelisk of the market cross, on whose steps travellers sit to wait for the buses that stop opposite it. The atmosphere is one of almost romantic permanence; here, you feel, are still to be found 'the good old days'.

This walk is over, but no visitor can leave Richmond without feeling that he or she has put out a hand to touch the living past. Do not fail to see the ruins of Richmond Castle from the riverside or, if you can find time, by walking around the castle grounds. The Castle keep was built in about 1150, the magnificent tower is 100 ft tall and has walls 11 ft thick. It is as strong and enduring as ever.

The Short Cut

Hawes to Thwaite & Muker over Great Shunner Fell

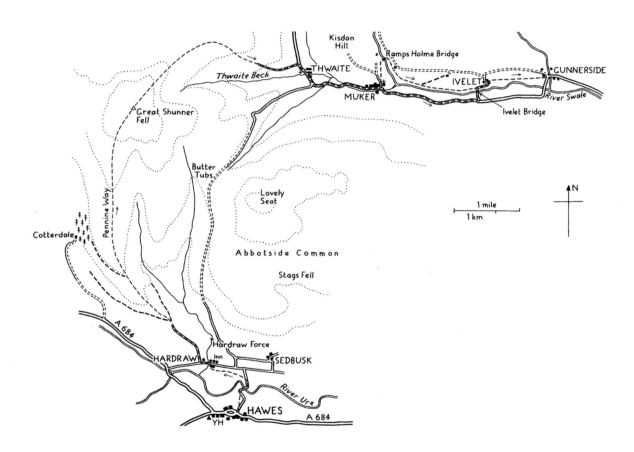

- ➤ *Distance:* About 10½ miles/16.8km (to Muker)
- ➤ *Altitude gained:* About 1600 ft/488m
- ➤ *Terrain:* Over high gritstone moorland, but most of the boggier stretches are now traversed by stone slabs so it is comparatively easy walking.
- ➤ *Refreshments:* At Hardraw, Thwaite and in Muker.

Great Shunner Fell seen from near Appersett ➤

As mentioned in the Introduction, it is possible to curtail the main walk and go directly to Swaledale from near the head of Wensleydale, linking Hawes with Thwaite via Great Shunner Fell, the route used by the Pennine Way, and then picking up the main route again at Muker. I do not recommend that anyone should omit the splendid Lady Anne Clifford's Highway, or Wild Boar Fell, or the Nine Standards, for they are some of the best parts of the whole walk but, if it is really necessary, it can be done. By continuing down Swaledale beyond Thwaite the overall time can be reduced by a day, or even two days, depending on overnight accommodation and the stamina of the walker. It is too complicated to describe all the variations possible, but a glance at the linear diagram of distances between places, in conjunction with your accommodation plans, should help – *see* page 125.)

As for accommodation, there is no conveniently situated Youth Hostel, except at

Keld, and that is three miles uphill in the wrong direction from Thwaite, but there are half a dozen places offering B&B accommodation between Thwaite and Gunnerside (the best guide to these is the *Coast to Coast Accommodation Guide; see* Introduction, page xii). It would seem sensible to make an advance booking from Hawes before setting off.

In addition to repeating that I do think it would be a great pity to miss out Days Three and Four of the main walk, I must also say emphatically that this short-cut route is not a low-level easy option. Great Shunner Fell stands at 2348 ft/716m above sea level (just higher than Wild Boar Fell) and it is exposed to bad weather like all the high Pennine fells.

Hawes to Hardraw

Assuming that you found accommodation in Hawes at the end of Day Two, the first part of the Short Cut is a reversal of the last part of the previous day's route. From the car park at the National Park Centre at the east end of Hawes (grid ref 876898), take the road to the north-east towards Sedbusk and Hardraw. In about 200 yds take a

stone-flagged path on the left, signed for the Pennine Way, which cuts off a corner. Rejoining the road, cross the River Ure by the double-arched Haylands Bridge and then take the second footpath on the left, at the top of a few steps, also signed 'Pennine Way'. This leads, with more flags, to Hardraw, reaching a stile and gate at the side of the café here, directly opposite the Green Dragon pub. If you did not visit the remarkable cascade of Hardraw Fells yesterday, now is your opportunity to do so, going through the pub premises: *see* page 41.

Hardraw to Great Shunner Fell

Leaving the Green Dragon, turn right (west) past the lych gate to the attractive parish church, cross the road bridge over the beck and pass Harris House, the Outdoor Centre for William Hulme's Grammar School, on the right. The first turn after that is a walled lane, with a finger-post pointing north-west and reading 'FP Thwaite 8 (PW)'. This is the continuation of the Pennine Way.

The track starts to climb almost immediately, curving left and passing a small stand of conifers. By looking over the wall on the right, a field away, you can see the wooded amphitheatre into which Hardraw Force pours with such grace. Beyond that is the best possible view of the terraces and grassed-over spoil-tips on the side of Stags Fell, from where so much stone was mined. Then, on a short level stretch of this walled lane, just before it bends right and up to the fell gate which terminates it, you have a view directly ahead to Cotter End. The wall rising up its crest, shadowed by Lady Anne Clifford's Highway, is clearly in view: that is the way you might have been going ... but it is a bit late now to have second thoughts.

Almost immediately beyond the gate the track forks, but the right-hand track is a dead end and you should follow a Pennine Way finger-post which points you to the left. Then, in a further 200 yds a second finger-post marks where a

The Green Dragon Inn, Hardraw ➤

◀ *Haylands Bridge over the River Ure; Stags Fell beyond*

faint, grassy trod veers off left towards Cotterdale. Our main track leads ahead, steadily rising, over open moor and along the crest of a broad ridge, passing closely by a wall enclosing land on the Cotterdale side and then rising more steeply to reach a gate and quite a large sheepfold. About 50 yds beyond the sheepfold the tracks fork again, the left-hand one signed 'BW Cotterdale 3km' and taking a traversing line. The right-hand fork is marked by a Pennine Way finger-post pointing NNW and the route confirmed by a couple of cairns seen ahead. There are now no more side tracks or paths to confuse the issue: it is just a straightforward plod ahead.

From being limestone down at the Hardraw level, the underlying rock is now undoubtedly gritstone and the path passes through a zone of embedded boulders and small outcrops, but at an easier angle. From here, looking over to the left, you may catch sight of a tall stone beacon, square-built and about 12 ft high. It needs a diversion to visit it, not only for a view over Cotterdale but also for a grand, if distant, view to the splendid edges of Wild Boar Fell, above Mallerstang. You can have a few more regrets that you have not gone that way today.

Back on the path after that diversion, it continues to climb gently uphill, passing a half-collapsed sheepfold but then crossing a boggy bit of land on some duck-boards. But whereas there used to be many such sections, from here over the top of the fell and onto the Swaledale side, most of them have now been replaced by stone flags, creating sections of causeway. I have heard that some walkers do not like these, feeling that the character of the ground underfoot is changed. While agreeing that this is certainly true, I can recall this track before there were any such 'causeys', and it was a nightmare, particularly on the Swaledale side. For a popular long-distance path such as this, I cannot see that there was any alternative. These flags are a traditional answer, can last (and have lasted elsewhere) for centuries and are infinitely preferable to the experiments with polypropylene web and duck-boards on stilts on parts of the Three Peaks Walk further south. The stone flags do quickly blend into the landscape and become part of it, while protecting it from erosion (which was particularly bad in places) and making the way plain.

Beyond the collapsed sheepfold, the line of the path can be seen, following the curve of the broad ridge ahead, closely by-passing another stone beacon and with sight of another further away. There were mineworkings up here, for coal I believe, and the many cairns (or 'stone men') and beacons must have been erected to help the miners find their way. Plodding along purposefully, just as they must have done, there should be no difficulty in reaching the great heap of stones, hollowed out to form a windbreak, on top of Great Shunner Fell. The views are wide-ranging, especially to the NE, towards Swaledale, and to the SE, where sharp eyes can distinguish more beacons and cairns on Lovely Seat, beyond the Butter Tubs Pass road.

Field bottoms outside Thwaite, seen from the end of the Pennine Way track ➤

Great Shunner Fell to Thwaite and Muker

Striking off to the north-east, the path leads in a wide curve along the high land to the north of the feeder streams flowing into Thwaite Beck, passing another beacon en route and, after about 1½ miles, begins a more noticeable descent to a gate at the end of the walled lane leading the last mile to join the B6270 road north of Thwaite. A right turn down the steep slope quickly leads into the village, and what you do now depends on the overnight accommodation you have either pre-booked or are contemplating. Kearton's well-known tea-house and restaurant here may well detain you anyway for some refreshment.

To pick up the route of the main walk again, Day Five from Keld to Reeth, you will need to walk firstly from Thwaite to Muker, and if you have dallied at Kearton's you will probably find it easiest to walk down the road for the mile or so that is needed. And if you are still in a hurry, you may just as well carry on along the road as far as Oxnop, the turn off on the left to Ivelet Bridge. On its other (N) side, you can walk into Ivelet and then pick up the last part of the walk into Gunnerside, as described on page 90 in Day Five.

If, however, time is not your enemy, it is scenically well worth heading *north* out of Muker to Ramps Holme Bridge, to pick up the very attractive footpath on the north bank of the River Swale. To do this, as you enter Muker from Thwaite, continue to the east end of the village but then turn left in front of the Literary Institute. The metalled road veers left in front of the post office, but here keep right to find a sign-post for Gunnerside and Keld. A stile by a gate leads to half a dozen more stiles across meadowland. Ramps Holme Bridge will come into sight but please do not cut across the pasture until the path you are on reaches the river bank, when you should turn right to reach the bridge. The OS map, incidentally, shows a right of way heading north-east out of Muker which looks as if it would nicely cut off the corner by crossing the Swale to link up with the path at Ramps Holme. It would probably be fine in a horse and trap; on foot you are likely to have to risk paddling.

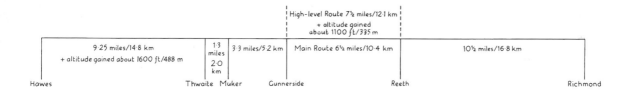

◄ Above *Thwaite, looking east along Thwaite Beck;* below *Muker, with Kisdon Hill behind*

Appendix

Three Circular Walks

The three walks described below are all circular walks starting and finishing at one of the overnight halts on the main walk. None is longer than 7½ miles/12km, a comfortable half-day's walk. In order that the walks can be used separately from the main walk, perhaps on a return visit to the Dales, they are written with that in mind and will inevitably contain some repetition with the main walk where the routes coincide.

Circular Walk: Aysgarth to the Templars Chapel

➤ *Best map:* OS 1:25 000 Outdoor Leisure 30 Yorkshire Dales Northern & Central Areas
➤ *Distance:* About 5¼ miles/8.4km
➤ *Height gained:* About 300 ft/91m
➤ *Time required:* About 2½ hours
➤ *Terrain:* On good paths with one short, usually muddy section.
➤ *Refreshments:* West Burton has a post office that sells sandwiches, and a pub, the Fox and Hounds. This would be a good place to stop for lunch.

This delightful short walk could easily form part of a visit to Aysgarth Falls, which are best approached from the Yorkshire Dales National Park Centre and car park, on the north side of the River Ure, from where signed paths lead visitors to the best viewing points. Aysgarth Falls is, however, a tourist 'honeypot', so it is advisable to choose one's time to visit.

Having done so, to start this walk, take the road (or the adjacent footpath) from the National Park Centre and go downhill to cross the River Ure by the road bridge just below High Force (or Falls, dependent on whether you use the OS name or the

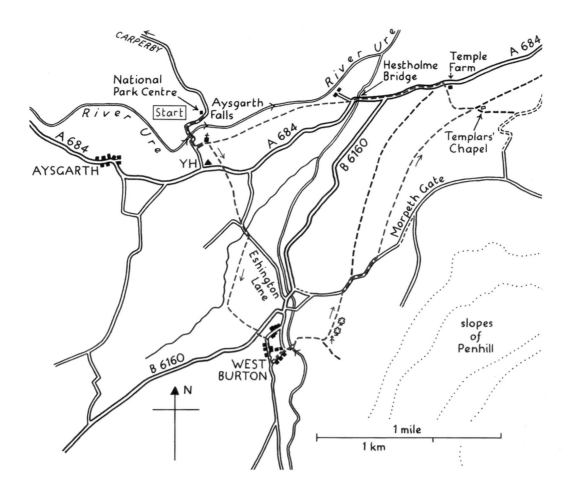

YDNP name) and continue uphill round the bend towards the A684. Halfway up the slope, turn left into the grounds of St Andrew's Church which is itself very well worth a visit (*see* page 14), then turn right directly opposite its front door. A metalled walk from here leads SSE between pollarded trees and up a further slope to reach the A684. Cross this to a gated stile opposite where there is a sign reading 'FP Eshington Bridge' and follow a trod sloping down a meadow to a second stile, with a view ahead to the houses and fields of West Burton, backed by the heights of Harland Hill and Penhill. A steeper descent down a grassy bank to a dip, a rise up the opposite slope and a further descent beyond it, with stiles and yellow arrows pointing the way, leads to the road at Eshington Bridge which crosses over Bishopdale Beck. On the other side of the bridge, take a footpath 50 yds further on, on the right, signed 'West Burton ¾ mile' which leads SSW across an almost perfectly flat meadow, grazed to a fine velvet turf by sheep and part of which is used for a football pitch. Beyond the next stile this path shadows the adjacent wall on the right, then changes direction to south-east at a stile and bend in the nearby Bishopdale Beck, crossing another field to a barn and continuing to some steps and a stile onto the B6160. You will be interested to note that the signpost here, pointing back the way you have just come, reads 'Eshington Bridge ½ mile' – which suggests that if you do this walk in the reverse direction it will be a quarter of a mile shorter . . .

Slanting rightwards across the road, more steps and a narrow passage lead into the village of West Burton, turning right to reach the attractive triangular green with its swings and stone cross topped by a wind vane. This is a delightful place to linger awhile, encouraged by the convenient seats placed strategically round the green, or tempted by the delicious smells emanating from the Fox and Hounds.

Leave the green from its north-east corner. As you do, you will hear the sound of falling water, quickly find the old stone footbridge over the Walden Beck and see the pretty cascade a few yards upstream, where it pours over an undercut sill shaded by trees. The footpath crosses the bridge, climbs the far bank to a gate and then up the edge of the pasture beyond, past a sign reading 'FP Barrack Wood', to reach a step-stile over a fence on the bottom edge of some woodland. A finger-post here points uphill, for 'Hudson Quarry Lane', and left (north-east) and initially slightly downhill for 'Morpeth Lane'. We are aiming for Morpeth Gate, so this is the way to go. A pleasant trod leads along the bottom edge of the wood, with good views over the dale below; then, on leaving the wood, it slants slightly downhill to join the walled gravel track of Morpeth Gate: 'gate', incidentally, is derived from the Nordic word *gatan* meaning 'lane'.

Turn right onto the track which turns uphill, continuing past a footpath signed for 'Temple Farm' at a gate on the left, to a bend, with a limestone scar showing ahead on the skyline. Here there is another gate on the left and another path, this time signed for 'Templars Chapel 1'. This delightful and little-used trod traverses the slopes overlooking the dale below, shortly rising to a gate and then contouring along the top edge of a grassy escarpment. The views get better as you go, with

Cauldron Force on Walden Beck, near West Burton

Aysgarth church tower becoming visible on the left (north-west) while, directly ahead, to the north-east, you should be able to see the pale stone fortress of Bolton Castle across Wensleydale. You reach a gated stile at a cross-wall below an old quarry and from then onwards the bank on the left is clothed with beech woods, so that the walking is along a wide, grassy shelf sloping up to a skyline crowned by the heights of Penhill on the right.

Penhill Preceptory of the Knights Templar is notable for the exposed and very puzzling stone coffins on show there; they look too small to have held ordinary human beings, let alone the corpses of gallant knights used to wielding heavy swords and carrying armour (*see* page 28).

Leaving the Preceptory, return to the stony lane and head back downhill and sharp left below the wooded escarpment towards Temple Farm (finger-post). This lane also acts as the conduit for any excess water draining from the slope above, so the approach to Temple Farm is frequently wet or muddy. Visually, the farm is a disaster, dominated by a huge silage tower and tyre-covered silage clamps so, with muddy boots and

averted eyes, you will be glad to join the main A684 via a slit-stile and turn left along it. Care is needed for a short way as there is little verge, but then you walk easily downhill and round the bends to reach Hestholme Bridge.

On its north side, a footpath is indicated on the right at the entrance to the drive to Hestholme Farm and a single-file trod from here now slants west across a level pasture towards the bank of the River Ure which can be heard if not yet seen. Two wicket-gates lead quickly to the margin, close by a series of small cascades, then the path starts to climb a slope and it becomes clear that the river, which is quite wide here and flowing over limestone pavement below, is emerging from a vertically-sided rocky gorge. Although the OS map shows the path splitting, with one branch going along the bank, it is in fact channelled by a fence so it climbs up the slope above and to the left of the gorge, probably to avoid the risk of accidents.

Aysgarth Lower Force, where the waters pour over four distinct rock lips, can be seen below, though not very well from this bank. The path leads into a small plantation of sycamores and you emerge to a fine view of St Andrew's Church again, across an adjacent meadow, and the path leads directly into its grounds.

Turn right outside the church's front door and the path leads directly to the road. Turn right here to go steeply downhill to cross the bridge (look left to see Aysgarth High Force) and so back to the car park. If you did not visit Middle and Lower Forces before you set out, now is the time to do so.

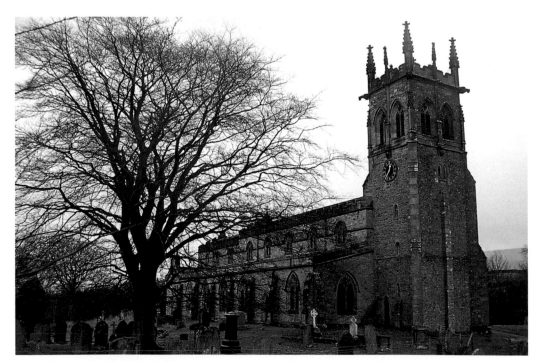

St Andrew's Church, Aysgarth

Circular Walk: Stags Fell and Pike Hill from Hawes

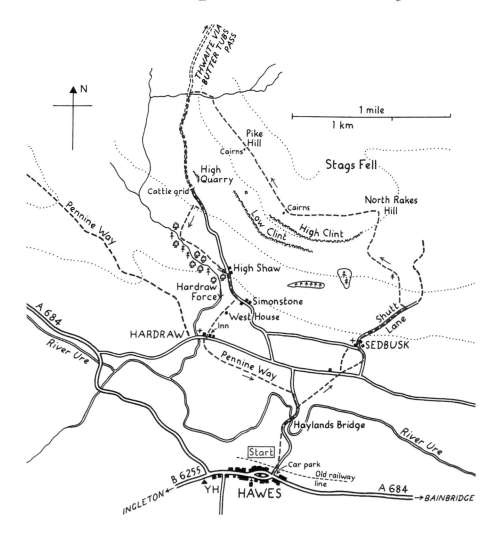

➤ *Best map:* OS 1:25 000 Outdoor Leisure 30 Yorkshire Dales Northern & Central areas

➤ *Distance:* About 7½ miles/12km

➤ *Height gained:* Approx. 984 ft/300m

➤ *Time required:* About 4½ hours

➤ *Terrain:* Apart from a little unavoidable tarmac, the walking is almost all on good paths over limestone and so is generally dry underfoot.

➤ *Refreshments:* It is advisable to stock up in Hawes before you set out since the only refreshments you will find are in Hardraw, very close to the end of the walk.

This circular walk gives some fine high-level views over Wensleydale and offers far more variety of landscape than might be inferred from a glance at the map. It can easily encompass a visit to the famous Hardraw Force at the end of the walk. There is a large car park at the National Park Centre at the east end of Hawes, just off the A684 (grid ref 876898). This is a convenient place (in both senses of the word) from which to start the walk.

Leave the car park either by turning right out of the entrance and then right again (north-east) onto the road to Hardraw and Sedbusk, or by crossing the old railway line by the bridge at the north-west corner of the car park and then turning right along the road. Very shortly a stile on the left leads onto a flagged path, signed for the Pennine Way, which cuts off a corner of road, rejoining it just before reaching the double-arched Haylands Bridge over the River Ure. From here you have a good view of Stags Fell rising ahead to the north and can gain a good idea of the walk ahead for it climbs the grassy slopes towards two well-defined limestone scars, the upper one of which appears to form the skyline; it then traverses that skyline from right to left.

Shortly after crossing the Ure, take a path signed 'Sedbusk ¾' at a stile on the right; this leads to a footbridge over an evil backwater and then climbs gently, via

two more stiles, to reach and cross the Hardraw–Askrigg road, with a stile immediately opposite. Two paths lead from here, but take the right-hand one up the field to a slit-stile (which is of the tight-fit ankle-cracking variety: you will have fun getting through this even if your legs are 5 feet long). The next stile, reached up a steeper slope, is thankfully easier and steps onto the tarmac lane leading into Sedbusk. Turn left onto this, curving left, then right and into Shutt Lane, passing a Primitive Methodist Chapel (1875) on the left to reach the small village green.

As you leave the village, turning uphill to the north-east into a walled lane and comforted by a signpost reading 'North Rakes Hill', the tarmac surface changes to one of concrete with grooves cut across it to give traction on the steep slope, but soon alters to gravel as the angle eases. After about ¼ mile, a metal gate bars the lane but there is a ladder-stile and gate on the left just before reaching it. These lead directly to a sunken green lane heading uphill to the north-west, but this soon curves right and peters out in the pasture and you continue instead by an obvious green pathway, heading north towards some ash and sycamore trees seen ahead.

As you climb this slope and reach the copse, you may notice that the stones of the crumbling enclosure which originally sheltered these trees from the nibbling teeth of sheep are gritstone and not limestone. Gritstone underlies limestone on much of Stags Fell and was extensively mined, as well as quarried, hundreds of tons being shipped by rail every month from Hawes at the end of the nineteenth century. The only evidences to be seen now, although out of sight from here at this point, are the terraces of spoil with their big cairns (stone men) which are on the south-west slope of Stags Fell. These will be more visible on the return half of the walk.

This lovely grass path curves left at the top edge of the copse, swinging north-west and rising to a gate in a transverse wall, with the light grey

The Primitive Methodist Chapel in Sedbusk

◄ *Sedbusk from the foot of Shutt Lane*

limestone scar of High Clint directly in view ahead. The way then slants across more pasture to another gate in the intake wall, beyond which is open moor. Looking back gives a grand panoramic view of almost the whole of Wensleydale.

Continuing uphill to the north, the trod swings slightly to the right round a low hummock to pass a finger-post above it then, at an easier angle, continues further to reach another finger-post reading 'Bridleway' and pointing back the way you have just come. You have clearly reached the top of the moor, the plateau, and this is North Rakes Hill – although there is not much that you or I would recognise as a hill. No problem; you are definitely in the right place so long as no one has nicked the last finger-post.

From here head left (west) on what is still a fairly well-defined path, and becomes more so, up a slight rise and onto an almost level grass-covered limestone plateau. If, like me, you were expecting a great view from here, you too will also be disappointed, for there is just a wide expanse of moor of heather and rough grass rising gently above the plateau. However, on the skyline ahead and to the west is an obvious large cairn looking like an upturned funnel, and an attractive green bridleway cuts right across the top of the plateau towards it. That is the route, but for a grand view over Hawes, the one you thought you were going to get earlier, go along it for only a couple of hundred yards and then turn off it temporarily, heading hard left, south, and you will reach the top of High Clint, the edge of the scarp. Here you'll get a sensational view, and a steady updraught in your face from the prevailing south-westerlies.

Return to the green way and follow it over the plateau. You will have to divert again slightly to the funnel-shaped cairn but it is worth it for a good view to Great Shunner Fell and Cotter End to the north-west. Nearby are two more substantial cairns, like pillars and 6–7 ft high; below, you can see a large multi-chambered sheepfold built beyond some indefinite limestone scars.

You should now return once more to the green way, to pass numerous shakeholes. After about ½ mile heading roughly north-west, it begins to trend slightly downhill and reaches another finger-post. The path now dips into an area of rushes and little outcrops and then rises again to some obvious cairns which mark Pike Hill. To the WNW more finger-posts can be seen and are useful because the path becomes very indistinct on stony ground, but then two more finger-posts are reached, one on each side of a shallow ravine with low limestone walls on either side. This is Shivery Gill and the guide-post on its far side points down a jeep track to the Butter Tubs road which runs between Hawes and Thwaite in Swaledale.

There is only a short descent to reach the road onto which you turn left downhill. It is easy walking along the grass beside the unfenced section until it crosses a cattle-

*Above Looking over Wensleydale to Widdale from High Clint;
below Cotter End, seen from the cairns at the west end of High Clint* ▶

grid after which it is then walled or fenced on both sides. On the descent you can look along the flank of the fell to the left to see the spoil-heaps of the former High Quarry, and the terraces and stone men mentioned earlier. Para-gliders have discovered the good conditions for their sport here and can often be seen floating silently in the thermals rising up the edge of the scarp.

When almost below a group of about ten stone cairns seen above, look for a finger-post by a slit-stile on the right, beside a gate and a finger-post reading 'FP High Shaw'. This leads to a barn about 50 yds away with a ladder-stile hidden behind it. Cross this and on its other side turn sharp left (yellow arrow) and head south-west downhill beside the wall. The descent leads to a stile at the edge of a wooded gill, the path continuing just inside its enclosed area which is left by another stile. A grassy path from here crosses several pastures to the SSE, giving easy walking towards some buildings ahead. These prove to be part of the hamlet of High Shaw and the path is signed past some of the buildings to join a wooded lane, where you turn left to rejoin the Butter Tubs road.

Turn right downhill and 30 yds before you reach the road sign for 'Simonstone',

take a right turn at a footpath sign (pointing through the local authority's road-materials yard) which leads directly to a farm track. This continues downhill to pass West House (farm) and then, on stone flags and steps, more steeply down a field to reach Hardraw. You reach the road right next to the Green Dragon pub and I dare say that the refreshments here, or at the tea shop opposite, will add to the pleasures of using this as an occasion to visit Hardraw Force, England's longest unbroken waterfalls above ground, which are reached through the Green Dragon's premises (*see* page 41).

To return to Hawes, cross the road from the Green Dragon to a gate and stile to the immediate right of the tea shop opposite. A finger-post here reads 'FP Brunt Acres Road (Pennine Way)' and within a few yards a second finger-post ('P. W.') points left (south-east). A narrow causeway of stone flags now marks the path away from farm buildings and across pastures and, when the flags end, an obvious good path continues across more fields, with stiles, to reach Brunt Acres Road at a stile and some steps.

Turn right here, crossing the River Ure again at Haylands Bridge and continue into Hawes, reversing the last bit of the outward walk.

Typical Dales fields near Hardraw

◄ *Overlooking Fossdale from the lower slopes of Stags Fell*

Circular Walk: Around the Hill of Kisdon

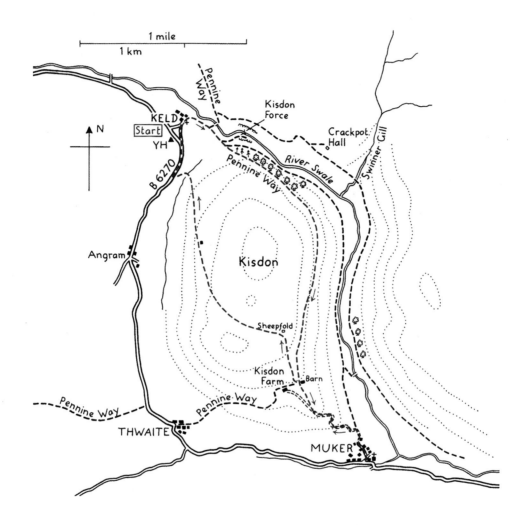

- ➤ *Best map:* OS 1:25 000 Outdoor Leisure 30 Yorkshire Dales Northern & Central Areas
- ➤ *Distance:* About 4 miles/6.4km (to continue to Muker and back – *see* text – adds about 1¾ miles/2.8km)
- ➤ *Height gained:* About 650 ft/198m (or about 1150 ft/351m if you go to Muker and back)
- ➤ *Time required:* About 2 hours (or about 3 hours if you go to Muker and back)
- ➤ *Terrain:* Almost all on good paths over well-drained limestone.
- ➤ *Refreshments:* None – unless you go to Muker.

Overlooking the Swale gorge from near Keld ➤

This walk around the hill of Kisdon is a delight. During the last Ice Age about 10,000 years ago, the River Swale changed course from the west side of Kisdon to the east, as glaciers deepened the valley which now forms the Swale gorge. The effect was to leave the hill of Kisdon shaped rather like a very broad upturned boat, with a rounded, flattened dome and particularly deep sides. To walk around Kisdon at a high level is, therefore, to enjoy a succession of grand views, enhanced by its comparative isolation.

From the irregularly-shaped square at the bottom of the slope in Keld and pointing to the right (east) out of it, is a finger-post reading 'Public footpath to Muker'. The route now leads out of Keld along a half-sunken lane. In about 250 yds and at a 'Pennine Way' finger-post, this lane turns off left, down to a footbridge over the River Swale. Instead of turning downhill, however, keep on the higher level, with views through vegetation over on the left to the cliffs of the Swale gorge, and in about 100 yds pass through a gate. In a further 150 yds there is a finger-post 'FP Kisdon Upper Force' pointing to the left where a path leads down to the finest of the Swale's many waterfalls, Kisdon Force. At the time of writing, however, because of land slippage, this route is rather tricky near to the river bank, and a better and safer way is suggested (*see* page 86).

Now, continue on the upper path for about 200 yds as it passes below a limestone

scar. Just before it reaches the top of a little rise, beyond which there is a clear view down to the Swale, veer to the right at a large cairn (there is also a Pennine Way finger-post, but at the last time of passing it lay supine on the ground and was not being very helpful) and, instead of descending, take a fairly narrow but rising path traversing the fellside to the south-east, and shortly pass through a gap in an intake wall.

The path now leads alongside this wall and just above it, with extensive woods of silver birch below which mask the views below for almost ½ mile or so. However, when the woods end, there are splendid views across the valley below to the ruins of Crackpot Hall, seen at the same level opposite, and then into Swinner Gill.

There is no risk of losing the path now as it continues to traverse the steep slope, through a slit-stile or gateway at the occasional transverse wall, crossing a few patches of limestone scree but otherwise along grassy ledges and with continuing grand views ahead down the valley on the left. In due course, the buildings of Muker come into sight again and the Swale now forms wide curves rather than cataracts. A ladder-stile and then a step-stile lead to where a barn, next to Kisdon Farm, comes into view ahead. Next to the barn there is a double-armed finger-post for the Pennine Way, with one arm pointing back the way we have just come and the other pointing to the right (west) towards Thwaite.

At this point you need to take the decision whether to descend the slope to Muker and the temptations of whatever fleshpots you may find there: a description of that option follows at the end of this chapter. To continue the walk without descending, the way we now go is the route taken by the old corpse road, turning back sharply northwards. It is not signed but a grassy trod goes up between the two arms of the Pennine Way, initially in a north-westerly direction and beside the wall climbing up the slope, half left. This path quickly leads into a walled lane heading north then, when the left-hand wall ends, continues upslope with a wall now on the right-hand side only. It leads towards a wall corner, with a sheepfold on the other side, but the path cuts across the corner, veering left (west) and rises onto a shoulder of Kisdon just below the highest land.

It passes through a gate and then a broad grass trod leads gently downhill to the north-west to reach another gate beyond which is a short section of collapsed walled lane. Open fellside follows to another gate where there is a finger-post 'Keld' and then a lovely stretch of velvety turf slants across the side of Kisdon, with fine views across the valley below to the barns and farmsteads of the hamlet of Angram. From here, a keen eye will also be able to pick out the cairn on the top of Great Shunner Fell (the continuation southwards of the Pennine Way) or the stone pillars atop the sprawling Lovely Seat, which is due south, above the Butter Tubs Pass road to Wensleydale.

Still declining gently, this delightful track passes just below an isolated house and then, with a wall now on the right-hand side and with the buildings of Keld in view ahead, goes more steeply down a stony track to the valley bottom. Here it swings left, crosses the little beck by a footbridge and climbs a walled lane to join the B6270 road uphill to the turn-off on the right into Keld. The circle is complete and so, I hope, will be your sense of satisfaction at the completion of this delightful walk.

The Muker Option

To continue down to Muker from the double-armed Pennine Way finger-post beside the barn close to Kisdon Farm, the direction is south-east. To the immediate right of the barn, a walled lane leads to a gate at its end and directly beyond it onto a gravel road which, as the slope steepens, becomes a tarmac strip. Following the tarmac downhill (it is a private road-cum-public footpath) it winds down to reach a gate and parking area for the houses just beyond. A metalled lane leads from here past the old vicarage and swings right in front of Muker's post office to reach the Literary Institute and the village centre. There is an excellent pub here, The Farmers Arms, and also a tea shop. Muker is well worth visiting.

For the return, reverse the last part of the downhill approach to the village, going

◄ *Barns, dry-stone walls and trees on the slopes of Kisdon Hill*

back up the metalled lane heading north, past the old vicarage, and up the tarmac strip once more – the short climb will help to keep you fit! Once it reaches the shoulder, the tarmac strip gives way to gravel; directly ahead now the barn can be seen once more, on the right, and the small farmhouse complex (Kisdon Farm) on the left. When the track turns sharp left through a gate to the farm, continue ahead up the gated and walled lane, emerging just left of the barn. Close by is the double-armed finger-post mentioned earlier, and the return route to Keld, via the old corpse road described above.

Muker: the Literary Institute

Index

Looking over Wensleydale from the two cairns west of High Clint

Route Directions

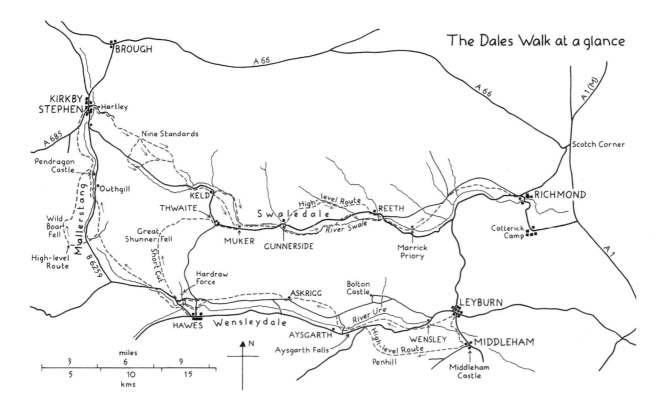

The Dales Walk at a glance

Useful Names, Addresses, Telephone Numbers

1. Youth Hostels Association National Office, 8 St Stephen's Hill, St Albans, Hertfordshire AL1 2DY.
   Tel. 01727-85515, fax. 01727-844126.
2. Youth Hostels Association Northern England Office, PO Box 11, Matlock, Derbyshire DE4 2XA. Tel. 01629-825850, fax. 01629-824571.
3. Yorkshire Dales National Park, Hebden Road, Grassington, Skipton, North Yorkshire BD23 5LB. Tel. 01756-752748, fax. 01756-752745.
4. YDNP Centre, Aysgarth Falls. Tel. 01969-663424.
5. YDNP Centre, Station Yard, Hawes. Tel. 01969-667450.
6. Richmond Tourist Information Centre, Friary Gardens, Victoria Road, Richmond, North Yorkshire. Tel. 01748-850252.
7. Leyburn Tourist Information Centre, Thornborough Hall, Leyburn, North Yorkshire. Tel. 01969-622773.
8. Kirkby Stephen Tourist Information Centre, Market Square, Kirkby Stephen, Cumbria CA17 4QN. Tel. 017683-71199.
9. Mrs Doreen Whitehead, East Stonesdale Farm, Keld, North Yorkshire DL11 6LJ. Tel. 01748-886374 (for 'Coast to Coast' Accommodation Guide etc).
10. Mr & Mrs Bowman, West View Farmhouse, Hartley, Kirkby Stephen, Cumbria CA17 4JH. Tel/fax. 017683-71680 (for 'Coast to Coast Pack Horse').
11. United Dalesbus: Tel. 01325-468771 (for up to date bus times in Wensleydale and Swaledale).
12. Some taxi operators in Richmond:
    D&J Taxis   01748-825112
    HK Taxis   01748-822323
    Trinity Cabs   01748-822269
13. Some taxi operators in Leyburn:
    BMW Taxis   01969-622604
    Elk Taxis   01969-622882
    G.A. Private Hire   01969-622790
14. A taxi operator in Hawes:
    Town Head Garage   01969-667483
15. Some taxi operators in Kirkby Stephen:
    J D Taxis   017683-71682
    John Thompson   017683-71741

Day One

Leyburn to Aysgarth

The first day has two quite separate routes, the main route on the lower level, and the high-level variation via Penhill. Both begin in Leyburn and join a short distance from Aysgarth, marching together at the end of the day.

Main (low-level) Route

- ➤ *Distance:* About 8 miles/12.8km
- ➤ *Altitude gained:* Negligible
- ➤ *Terrain:* The walking is mostly on the level over well-drained underlying limestone pastures.
- ➤ *Refreshments:* Leyburn is the place to stock up before starting the walk; the only other possibility may be in Wensley, but that is only half an hour's walk from Leyburn.

The route is slightly downhill from Leyburn by field paths to reach the River Ure at Wensley Bridge, with stiles and yellow arrows showing the way. From here it follows the course of the river upstream, staying mostly close to the south bank, passing Redmire Force, to Aysgarth. Finger-posts and stiles confirm the route beyond Wensley Bridge; if in doubt keep as close as possible to the river bank without climbing walls or fences.

Leyburn to Wensley

1. Leave Leyburn's Market Place opposite the Bolton Arms Hotel on the A684 signed for Wensley, Aysgarth Falls and Hawes. In about 150 yds look for a footpath sign on the left, pointing half-left (SW) across a field.

2. The way (often unclear on the ground) crosses the railway line by ladder-stiles, then two more stiles close together lead into a large field. Turn right along its top edge and use slit-stiles seen ahead to pass a

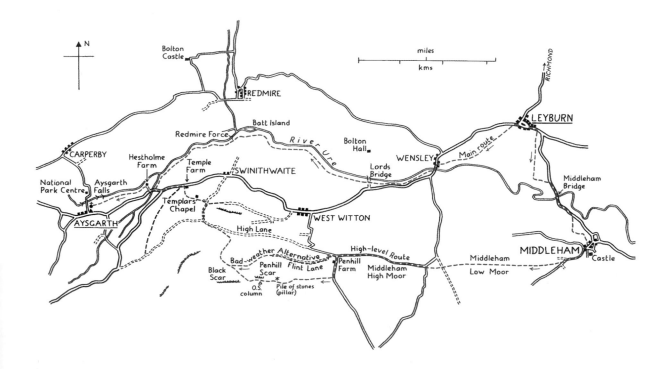

dilapidated barn on its left, then reach a gate beside pitches used by Wensleydale RUFC.

3. After the next stile, beside a cattle-trough, turn sharp left for 100 yds then right again, regaining the SW direction. Heading for a small plantation, the wall above it and on its right is crossed by a stile; then turn left and right to follow the left edge of the field and walk parallel to the River Ure now seen below.

4. A last stile into a paddock in front of a square-built detached house leads to a gate onto a metalled lane. Turn left here and downhill, turning right on reaching the road; Wensley Church will be opposite.

5. From the church turn left at the A684 to reach Wensley Bridge where it crosses the River Ure.

Wensley to Lords Bridge

1. From Wensley Bridge take a well-used if at times narrow footpath (finger-post) immediately over the bridge on the right. This shadows the river bank, heading upstream (generally W) through woodland to an open area, then through a young plantation of oaks and up to a gate on slightly higher ground.

2. Bearing right, a slit-stile just ahead gives access to the private drive (public footpath) crossing the Ure by Lords Bridge to Bolton Hall.

Lords Bridge to Redmire Force

1. Cross the drive by a slit-stile on the far side and take a faint green path across level pastures via slit-stiles to a gate beyond which a footbridge crosses a small stream.

2. At a finger-post immediately after, take the right fork, signed 'Hestholme Br for West Burton & Aysgarth', leading over another stile and back to the banks of the river. Delightful and easy walking follows through pleasant parkland, passing by the wooded Batt Island, where the river divides, then cutting across a wide bend to a point opposite the village of Redmire, not visible behind woodland.

3. The way now crosses otherwise level ground covered in small hummocks (a huge rabbit warren?), then rises to cross an area of much larger grass-covered lime-stone hummocks, running parallel to a tractor track from the buildings at Swini-thwaite, on the left, and reaching a ladder-stile over a wall where there is a notice put up by the Countryside Commission (now organised by the Min. of Ag.) about the Countryside Stewardship Scheme.

4. At the far side of the field beyond look for a finger-post and gate leading into the wood, to reach the river bank above the cataracts of Redmire Force.

Redmire Force to Aysgarth

1. The path leads down to the river bank at the upper cascade, then a made path, with steps, climbs back to the upper level. Slit-stiles now point the way across more pastures of almost level walking; watch for a fine view across the river to Bolton Castle.

2. More slit-stiles and finger-posts lead towards Wellclose Plantation but ensure you keep well right alongside the wall and fence to find the stile and finger-post directing you back down the slope on the right and beneath the trees to the river bank again at the ford of Slapestone Wath (a notice advises that the ford is dangerous and impassable).

3. Crossing more stiles, the way trends slightly away from the river bank and, via a ladder-stile, passes in front of the renovated house

at Adam Bottoms to a seven-barred metal gate just beyond it.

4. A level course across the field ahead, with the Walden Beck (a tributary of the Ure) now on the right-hand side, leads via a stile to another stile at the point where you step onto the tarmac of the A684. Turn right here to cross Walden Beck at Hestholme Bridge.

5. On its far side a finger-post on the right points across pastures (at the entrance to the drive to Hestholme Farm) towards the River Ure, reaching its bank via two wicket-gates and just before the cataracts of Lower Force.

6. The path runs beside the river for a short way, then the OS map shows the path split-ting, with one branch going along the bank; it is in fact channelled by a fence up the left bank and away from the gorge, probably to avoid the risk of accidents. In consequence the major cascades of Aysgarth Falls are not seen clearly.

7. The path now passes through a small syca-more plantation and then through the ground of St Andrew's Church.

8. The road is reached on the far side of the church and you turn uphill for the Youth Hostel (on the left at the junction with the A684 ahead), going right at the junction for the village, for the shop and for other accommodation. Turn downhill to cross the river by Yore Bridge to view the spec-tacular falls.

High-level Variation via Penhill

- *Distance:* About 12½ miles/20km
- *Altitude gained:* About 1400 ft/427m
- *Terrain:* **Mostly on well-drained grassy limestone shelves with a short section of road walking, and some peatier ground on the gritstone moorland of Penhill.**
- *Refreshments:* **Leyburn is the best place to stock up before starting the walk. Although there are tea shops and pubs in Middleham, it is only a short way from Leyburn. Thereafter, there are no facilities until you reach Aysgarth Falls.**

From Leyburn the route follows field paths towards a crossing of the River Ure at Middle-ham Bridge, and shortly into Middleham it-self. The route next traverses Middleham Low Moor, then the High Moor to Penhill Farm, beyond which it climbs to Penhill, the best viewpoint in Wensleydale. It contours west-wards above Penhill Scar then descends to the old Penhill Quarry to join High Lane and visit the Templars Chapel before the last leg into Aysgarth.

Leyburn to Middleham

1. Turn south-east in Leyburn's Market Place on the A684 towards Bedale and North-allerton to find the square-towered St Matthew's Church 50 yds beyond the point where the market place narrows to the width of the main road.

2. Directly opposite the church a 'public footpath' finger-post points south down a metalled path which almost immedi-ately crosses the railway line. It turns right, then left, down steps on the far side, passes the entrance to a bungalow and continues south between houses.

3. Reaching a metalled road in a small hous-

ing estate, turn right and sharp left through a slit-stile and, following yellow arrows, follow a grassy trod, always S, down two pastures via gateways and into a narrow field with trees, a small stream (forded on stones) and a stile at its far end.

4. Continue down the next pasture, keeping south and to the right alongside the fence, to another stile in the field corner. Beyond this a short descent leads to a junction with the metalled Low Lane. (Ignore an apparent short cut going left on the OS map to the bottom of Mighten's Bank.)

5. Turn left to the junction with the A6108, then right to reach and cross the River Ure by Middleham Bridge. Continue along the A6108 towards Middleham until some bungalows are reached on the right.

6. After the second bungalow, a finger-post 'public footpath' sign, on the right, leads over a wall by a short ladder-stile to a gate into a sloping field immediately beyond.

7. Turn left (arrows) and then curve right (S) up the sloping pastures and, via stiles at two field boundaries, reach a very substantial wall 50 yds before reaching more houses. Turn left (arrows) beside the wall and the path leads to a tarmac road at the edge of a small housing estate.

8. Turn half-right here and more arrows mark a good path passing behind more houses and, via two slit-stiles, into the grounds of the square-towered parish church.

9. Just before reaching the church, turn half-right at a war memorial into a narrow, paved passage between a high wall and some houses. When it ends at a minor road, go half-left: Middleham Castle ruins will be seen directly ahead. From the open space in front of the Castle turn left for the adjacent market place and refreshment possibilities. The castle is run by English Heritage and open 10 a.m. to 4 p.m. during the summer season, and at other times off-season.

Middleham to Penhill Farm

1. Leave Middleham by the walled Coverdale road, uphill to the SW, next to the castle ruins. When the walls end, continue a further 70 yds to where cars pull in on the right.

2. Leave the tarmac here, heading up a gently sloping grassy moor to the west, for safety keeping 30 yds left of a man-made gallops of raked sand and grit used by racehorses; there is little sign on the ground of the public bridleway here. The bulk of Penhill comes into view on the skyline to the W ahead.

3. Once past the point where the gallops end and the horses turn, you will spot a standing stone about 100 yds away on the right and in a further 150 yds will see a trig point on this flattened top (Cross Bank). Continue west for about ¾ mile to cross a gravel track and then reach a three-way road junction.

4. Continue along the road heading W (Common Lane) as far as the next junction at Penhill Farm.

Penhill Farm to High Lane via Penhill Scar

➤ (For a bad-weather alternative route, *see* page 154.)

1. For the normal high-level route, turn left here, uphill, on the Melmerby–Carlton road, leaving it 50 yds before reaching the gates and cattle-grid at the top of the rise for a gate and bridleway ('BW Penhill') on the right.

2. A grassy track, becoming more obvious across rougher pasture, leads via gates and gateways and eventually up pocket-steps in a last steep slope to reach the huge two-stepped cairn (the OS map's 'Pile of Stones') on Penhill's broad top.

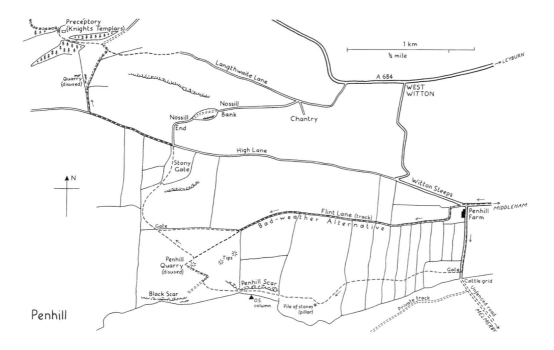

Penhill

3. Leave this heading NW, then almost immediately swinging west, along the edge of the escarpment overlooking Wensleydale, passing through a slit-stile as you approach the outcropping crags of Penhill Scar. Follow the escarpment until you have passed through a gap between the wall on the left and a wire fence on the right. Do not cross the main wall on the left onto the level moor which shelters numerous moorland birds, but continue in a W direction along the edge. It soon fades and becomes a steep convex slope, but use any of several trods to make towards the next outcropping crags of Black Scar.

4. Some 200–300 yds *before reaching* Black Scar, turn to the NW, half-right, down the convex slope, avoiding any rock outcrops, to intersect with a deep-cut man-made grassy groove, which slants back across the slope in a NE direction.

5. Follow the zigzags of this groove downhill to easier-angled ground at the level of

some obvious grassed-over spoil-tips (the site of the former Penhill Quarry). The green track, once at this level, leads NE towards a field corner (where Flint Lane enters the huge open field at the bottom of the steep slopes of Penhill) but watch for cairns indicating a narrow trod heading sharp left (NW) across this rough pasture to reach a gate in the lower enclosing wall (grid ref 043873; the nearest wall corner should be then about 120 yds away on your left).

6. Beyond this gate (a YDNP notice on its other side asks that you close it), a grassy track leads left and then curves back right below a small limestone escarpment (passing a 'footpath' finger-post) and reaches another gate with a wicket-gate next to it.

7. Go through and curve left beyond it and down a grooved grassy track (Stony Gate) to reach a gate onto the walled High Lane. (Another walled lane, leading to Nossill End, Nossill Bank etc is directly opposite but is not the way to go.)

Bad-weather alternative route, avoiding Penhill

In the event of bad weather ahead on Penhill, at Penhill Farm road junction do not turn uphill but go straight across, just right of the farm buildings, to enter the narrow-walled Flint Lane heading W (finger-post 'FP Penhill Quarry 1'). This traverses the slopes below Penhill and just over 1 mile after leaving Penhill Farm the walls end where it turns into a huge pasture whose slopes rise on the left to the heights of Penhill. The old spoil-tips of Penhill Quarry are very evident. Continue W along a grassy track with the wall on your immediate right for 700 yds to find a gate piercing the wall. Turn right through this. You are now at (6) above.

High Lane to Aysgarth via the Templar Chapel

1. Turn left (W) along this almost level track for just under ½ a mile, then turn right at the next walled track. In 200 yds, after a bend with a roofless barn on the corner, this track becomes a concrete slope, then levels, then descends again as a concrete slope, passing a finger-post reading 'FP Nossill Lane 1 via Langthwaite Lane'.
2. On the final bend (as the track turns back sharp right) leave it to go left (W) and down a grassy track which funnels you between two enclosed patches of woodland to a gate in the bottom corner.
3. Beyond this gate a track leads down another

pasture to the fenced enclosure containing the Penhill Preceptory, the Knights Templar Chapel.

4. A slit-stile next to the Preceptory (sign 'FP Temple Farm ¼' leads into a rough lane overhung with trees and slanting down to a gate and muddy track towards Penhill Farm, reaching the main A684 road at a slit-stile.
5. Turn left here and downhill, past the junction of the B6160, to cross Walden Beck at Hestholme Bridge.
6. On its far side, a finger-post on the right points across pastures (at the entrance to the drive to Hestholme Farm) towards the River Ure, reaching its bank via two wicket-gates, and just before the cataracts of Lower Force.
7. The path runs beside the river for a short way, then the OS map shows the path splitting, with one branch going along the bank; it is in fact channelled by a fence up the left bank and away from the gorge, probably to avoid the risk of accidents. In consequence the major cascades of Aysgarth Falls are not seen clearly.
8. The path now passes through a small sycamore plantation and then through the grounds of St Andrew's Church.
9. The road is reached on the far side of the church and you turn uphill for the Youth Hostel (on the left at the junction with the A684 ahead) going right at the junction for the village, for the shop and for other accommodation. Turn downhill to cross the river by Yore Bridge to view the spectacular falls.

Day Two

Aysgarth to Hawes

- ➤ *Distance:* About 12½ miles/20km
- ➤ *Altitude gained:* About 575 ft/175m
- ➤ *Terrain:* Occasionally muddy, but almost all on good tracks or paths, mostly well drained.
- ➤ *Refreshments:* Good choice in Askrigg and Hardraw.

The route transfers to limestone shelves and ledges at medium level on the north side of Wensleydale, linking Carperby with Askrigg and Sedbusk and visits Hardraw Force before ending at Hawes.

Aysgarth to Carperby

1. From Aysgarth village, or the Youth Hostel, turn downhill past St Andrew's Church towards Aysgarth Falls and Carperby, cross-ing the River Ure, with the High Force visible over the wall on the left.

2. Turn left through a kissing-gate to a tarmac path signed for 'National Park Centre' but by-pass its car park and continue up some steps to cross the embankment of the former Wensleydale Railway via a kissing-gate.

3. The path leads north across meadows, over two stiles, to a gate onto the road but stay on the edge of the field beside the wall until a last slit-stile leads to the road on the outskirts of Carperby. Turn left at the road and then right at the junction into the village.

Carperby to Askrigg

1. In about 50 yds turn left (at the near (W) end of the village green), at a double finger-post pointing NW and reading 'To other paths ½ mile'. In 50 yds another finger-post 'Oxclose' confirms the direction, then a stile seen ahead over a wall (with a shippon on the left) leads into a walled and wide grassy lane.

2. At the gateway ahead up the slope, bear left (W) to a slit-stile leading onto a farm track

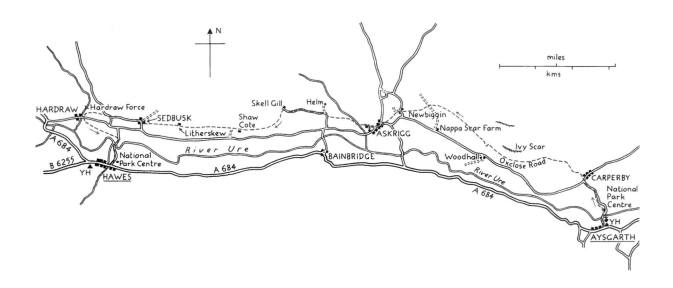

which is followed to the right (NW) to a metal gate at the top of a slight bend where it intersects with another track.

3. Turn left, climbing slightly, shortly passing through an old quarry, with abandoned stone slabs still piled on the left. A grass track curves onto the top of a limestone shelf and then turns left through a gateway into a large field.

4. Cross this to the W to a gateway with the lovely green way of Oxclose Road stretching onwards below limestone scars. This track shortly skirts old lead-mine spoil, becoming more of a jeep track as it crosses Thackthwaite Beck by a ford, just above a little waterfall.

5. Stay on the track as it turns through a gate ahead and downhill towards Woodhall, but turn back sharp right (NW) after only 10 yds and follow another obvious track to a gateway ahead.

6. The way is now obvious again, continuing NW, although rather rutted until some sheep-pens have been passed, then it once more becomes a lovely green sward, passing below the conifer plantation of The Coombs and then joining a walled lane at a gate beside a barn.

7. Follow the lane for 100 yds, ignoring a metalled track on the left but then turning left through a slit-stile onto a footpath leading to a mixed wood just down the slope. Follow the path through the wood, then to the top side of farm buildings and by slit-stiles across pastures to the hamlet of Newbiggin.

8. Passing between the houses, take a walled track just beyond the tiny green (heading SW) and in about 70 yds, just before it turns through a gate, take a slit-stile on the left. This leads to a barn, then slit-stiles beyond lead steeply down meadows (Stony Bank) to join a road just N of Askrigg, turning left downhill and into the village.

Askrigg to Skell Gill

1. Turn right at the Leyburn–Hawes road which leads into the market place with its village cross and take a metalled road just to the right of St Oswald's Church, where there is a sign 'Footpath Mill Gill Force'.

2. This leads W out of Askrigg then, just before the gateway to Mill Gill House, slants right on a stone-flagged path which leads to Mill Gill. Crossing the beck by a narrow footbridge, turn right up the left edge of the wooded gill to a junction of paths.

3. Mill Gill Force is only 200 yds or so along the right fork and worth seeing, then return to the junction and continue up the edge of the gill in the direction of Whitfield Gill (finger-post).

4. In about 100 yds leave this path at a finger-post signed 'FP Helm ½', going left at a slit-stile and away from the gill. The way (no clear path) leads uphill beside a wall on the right, going W, through a slit-stile ahead and continuing in that direction (W), crossing some open pasture to a junction of tarmac roads (at the end of the drive to the house of Helm).

5. Cross at the junction, going W along Skell Gill Lane, passing Lukes House on the left just before entering the hamlet of Skell Gill.

Skell Gill to Sedbusk

1. Leaving the hamlet, the tarmac ends and the road becomes a walled lane going round two bends. Keep left when it forks just before a ford to reach a gate beside sheep pens, then continue, with the wall now on the left side only, to the top of the rise just beyond. Here leave the track and curve half-right (SW) across pasture (with no clear path) but very quickly

reaching a green way just above a wall running W.

2. The way ahead is now straightforward for about 1½ miles, the grass becoming a gravel track as it passes barns and then the farm buildings at Shaw Cote.

3. Just beyond the farm the way leads into a walled lane. In about 150 yds turn off it at a slit-stile with a gate beside it on the right to follow a lovely footpath, marked by slit-stiles.

4. From the last slit-stile go towards Litherskew ahead, trending slightly right and left to spot a slit-stile just left of a collapsed building on the far side of the hamlet. More slit-stiles continue across delightful meadows to reach Sedbusk, keeping left on the approach to pass through a narrow strip of trees and reach the village on a bend in the road.

A typical Dales meadow, near Sedbusk

Sedbusk to Hardraw

1. Join the road, bearing slightly right, then, passing Rose Cottage and then Nether House on the right, continue going W along the narrow walled and metalled Sedbusk Lane.

2. At the junction (with the Butter Tubs Pass road) go straight across (finger-post 'FP Hardraw ¼') and follow a narrow path at the bottom of a wooded bank, leaving the wood at a stile and continuing across more open ground to another stile from where the village of Hardraw comes into view ahead.

3. Follow an obvious trod, via another stile, curving left into the village. Reaching the road between buildings, turn right immediately to enter the premises of the Green Dragon Inn, the only way to view Hardraw Force.

Hardraw to Hawes

1. Leaving the Green Dragon Inn, cross the road towards the tea shop opposite and take a path, starting at a gate and stile immediately right of the building. A finger-post here reads 'FP Brunt Acres Road (Pennine Way)' and within a few yards another finger-post ('P.W.') points left (SE). A narrow causeway of stone flags now marks the path away from farm buildings and across pastures.

2. When the causeway ends after three stiles, an obvious good path continues across more fields, with more stiles, to reach Brunt Acres Road at a stile and some steps.

3. Turn right along the road towards Hawes, crossing the River Ure by Haylands Bridge. Shortly after, watch for a flagged footpath on the right (signed for the Pennine Way) which cuts a corner into Hawes.

Day Three

Hawes to Kirkby Stephen

➤ *Distance:* About 15½ miles/24.8km on main route (high-level variation: about 19½ miles/31.2km)

➤ *Altitude gained:* About 850 ft/259m on main route (high-level variation: about 2350 ft/716m)

➤ *Terrain:* A bit of tarmac, otherwise grassy paths, mostly along high-level limestone shelves. (On the high-level variation there are sometimes boggy slopes to gain the high land, after which the going is good.)

➤ *Refreshments:* It is advisable to carry supplies with you although there are lunchtime possibilities at The Thrang. (On the high-level variation, there is a good tea room/café at Aisgill Moor Cottages.)

The first part of the day's walking, as far as Hell Gill Bridge, is common to both the main route and the high-level variation and involves a steady climb to Cotter End followed by a long traverse on grassy limestone shelves. The main route thereafter gently descends to the Mallerstang valley, following the course of the River Eden to the ruins of Pendragon Castle and then Lammerside Castle to reach Kirkby Stephen. The high-level variation leaves the main route at Hell Gill Bridge to traverse Swarth Fell and Wild Boar Fell.

Hawes to Cotter End

1. Leave Hawes by the A684 but as soon as Widdale Beck is crossed in Appersett take a footpath on the left signed 'Mossdale Head' which shadows the road to New Bridge and then follows the River Ure upstream until it reaches a farm track where you turn right to rejoin the A684.

continued p. 161

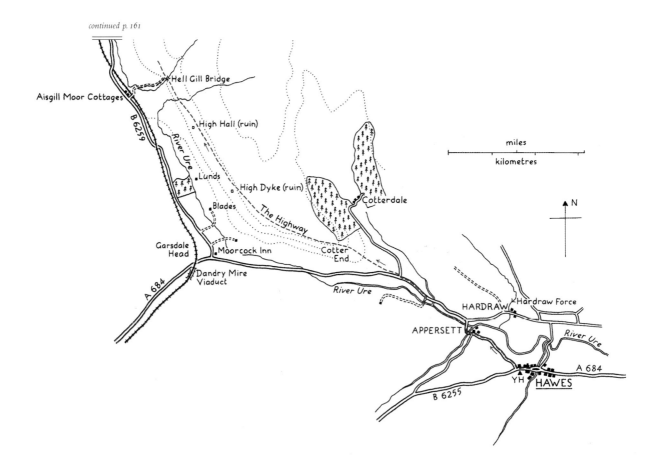

2. Turn left and walk slightly uphill to reach the minor road 'Cotterdale only' on the right.

3. This junction is the start of Lady Anne Clifford's Highway and a finger-post points NW up the spur of the broad grassy ridge ahead. The path soon shadows a wall, passes through a gate in a transverse wall almost on the brow of the ridge to reach Cotter End (the name presumably referring to the steep blunt end of the ridge).

Cotter End to Hell Gill Bridge

1. Here the path, becoming now a green way with a wall on the left, begins a long high-level traverse of a limestone escarpment.

2. After about ¾ mile, having passed through a gate at a transverse wall, the ruins of High Dyke are passed on the left, then, in about 1 mile further, those of High Hall.

3. In a further ½ mile you will, probably without realising it, cross the headwaters of the infant River Ure and in ¼ mile further still, now on an indefinite track on open fellside but with the trees in Hellgill clearly showing ahead, reach Hell Gill Bridge crossing a narrow gorge (Hellgill) containing the infant River Eden.

At this point, the high-level variation turns west to make a 1500 ft/457m ascent then a traverse of Swarth Fell and Wild Boar Fell before descending to rejoin the main route at Pendragon Castle (*see* page 161 for details). In poor visibility or conditions, the main route may prove better.

Hell Gill Bridge to The Thrang

1. Continue N from Hell Gill Bridge along the Highway, which rises gently until the wall on the left turns sharply downhill.

2. The track begins to decline across open fellside below the escarpments of Mallerstang Edge, reaching the B6259 at The Thrang Country Hotel (refreshments advertised).

The Thrang to near Shoregill

1. Immediately before reaching The Thrang Country Hotel, turn left at a sign for 'Deep Gill' and bear round right to cross Thrang Bridge.

2. Follow the left bank of the River Eden closely, over a stile and then (ignoring a farm bridge supported on girders) to a gate leading to farm buildings (part of Sycamore Tree Farm).

3. At a metalled track at the far side of the buildings, turn right through a gateway on a farm track leading to a bridge over the River Eden.

4. Before reaching the bridge, with tall yews and the bell-tower of Outhgill Church visible ¼ mile ahead, turn left (finger-post) on a faint trod across pasture on the left to a slit-stile. A faint path continues along the heavily wooded left bank of the river to reach a bridge bringing the track to Shoregill (buildings just out of sight) from the valley road.

From near Shoregill to Pendragon Castle

Here, at this bridge, you have a choice to make. Either cross the bridge and go to Pendragon Castle via Outhgill Church and the B6259, or continue into Shoregill and take field paths to the castle. Both routes are about the same length and at the same level. In rain, or when conditions are wet underfoot, the road route would be better. The field paths are kinder to your feet but a little slower.

To Pendragon Castle by Outhgill Church and the B6259

1. Cross the bridge, turn immediately left along the right bank (downstream) and follow a field path across a ditch and through a gap in a wall leading directly to Outhgill Church.
2. From here join the B6259 road and walk along it to Pendragon Castle.

To Pendragon Castle via Shoregill and the field path

1. Continue along the gravel track into Shoregill. In front of the last building (the post office) on the left, where there is a sign 'Pendragon Castle and Kirkby Stephen', turn right through several gates close together, the last one having a step-stile on its right-hand side, leading into a walled track (although the left wall is collapsed.)
2. At its end, following orange paint blobs, go half-left to a step-stile, half-left again to a second beside a gate and then slant half-left up a field track beyond.
3. Cross an iron stile and then an easy ford across Moss Gill (dilapidated barn up on left here). Paint blobs now cease but cross pasture ahead over a slight rise to a step-stile found in the wall ahead, crossing Riggs Gill immediately beyond.
4. Now bear right to another barn and turn right through the gate just past it, turning left along more pasture and now close to the River Eden again.
5. With Pendragon Castle visible directly ahead, cross another little gill and approach the house of Cocklake.
6. Here a sign reading 'goat-proof dog door' beside a stile marks the way; follow signs around the left edge of a paddock, reaching a road (Tommy Road) at a gate just a few

yards from Castle Bridge over the Eden. Here turn right to view the castle, just a few yards up the road.

Pendragon Castle to Lammerside Castle

1. Take the minor road (Tommy Road) signed 'Ravenstonedale 4' and follow the road round to cross the River Eden at Castle Bridge. Continue to pass a house called 'Cocklake' on a sharp bend and continue to a cattle-grid, after which the now unfenced road continues over open fell.
2. Immediately beyond the cattle-grid, bear right at a finger-post pointing N and signed 'Public Bridleway Wharton'. A good gravel track quickly becomes a green way, curving round the slope of Birkett Common.
3. When almost opposite Dalefoot Farm on the other side of the river, bear left (W) at a telegraph pole and follow the track, cutting across a bend in the river and then close by it again, with the ruins of Lammerside Castle now in view ahead.
4. Go through a gate, with the farm of Croop House now visible up to the left, but turn right immediately through another gate and cross pasture (faint path only) to the ruined Lammerside Castle.

Lammerside Castle to Kirkby Stephen

1. Go through a metal gate ahead, to the right of the ruins, and slant rightwards across the pasture beyond to another gate in the field corner, close to the river again.
2. Cross an adjacent fenced-off dry gill, leaving by a gate on its far side, then trend slightly left up the slope beyond to a gate at its top, from where the tower and buildings of Wharton Hall can be seen ahead.

3. Follow the fence on the right side of the next field, curving left at its end, where it is bordered by a wooded gill containing Mire Close Bridge, to reach a gateway and a concrete track.

4. Turn right here, passing through the com-

plex of farm buildings at Wharton Hall, and continue beyond them on the same track to reach the main A685 where a right turn leads directly into Kirkby Stephen where the Youth Hostel will be found in the centre of the small town.

High-level Variation: Hell Gill Bridge to Pendragon Castle via Swarth Fell and Wild Boar Fell

Note: This high-level route is about 4 miles/ 6.4km further than the main low-level route and has an extra altitude gain of about 1500 ft/457m.

Hell Gill Bridge to Aisgill Moor Cottages

1. Turning left through the gate on the N side of Hell Gill Bridge a good farm track leads downhill past Hellgill Farm, where the River Eden emerges from its ravine.

2. Continue through one gate and then another, where the track crosses the river

by a bridge, following it round left (immediately before reaching Hellgill Force) to cross the Settle–Carlisle railway at its highest point, Aisgill Moor Cottages, where refreshments are usually available.

Aisgill Moor Cottages to The Nab on Wild Boar Fell

1. Cross the B6259 road to a gate opposite (finger-post for 'Grisedale' *but ignore this*) and head uphill, just south of west, keeping left of the shallow groove of Smithy Gill.

2. The faint path roughly follows the county boundary, past a single large isolated boulder, with a last pull up to cairns on top of Swarth Fell Pike.

3. Turn right along the gritstone edge to

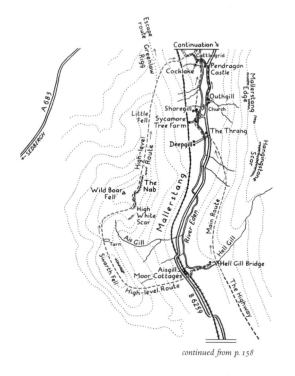

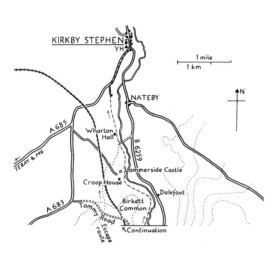

continued from p. 158

more cairns at the N end then follow a fair path N downhill towards the depression between Swarth Fell and Wild Boar Fell.

4. Shortly after passing a stagnant tarn in the depression, when the main path goes forward onto the top of the plateau, *veer right when the path forks*, walking NE and curving round The Band, the depression or combe drained by Ais Gill, to reach the fine escarpment of High White Scar overlooking Mallerstang. There are usually four or five large cairns here.

5. Continue along the edge of the escarpment to reach The Nab, where there is a single cairn.

The Nab to Tommy Road and Pendragon Castle

1. Descend the slope beyond, keeping fairly close to the edge (Scriddles), where there is a clear path, to a small windbreak and, about ¼ mile further on, to reach a wall corner where land is enclosed on the Ravenstonedale slope, on the left.

2. Follow the grassy path, with the wall on the left, to a dip after which the wall turns away left and the path rises gently to Little Fell. Here there are five or six cairns in line, with a solitary one on the highest point 70 yds further on.

3. Follow the grassy track down the slope beyond. After about 600 yds a wall appears on the right, enclosing land on the Mallerstang slope, and the angle of descent steepens.

4. The track shortly forks, the main track (the left branch) continuing ahead. *Do not follow this track* – unless you need to take the shortest possible route, in which case *see* opposite.

5. Instead follow the less well-defined right-hand trod, shadowing the wall on the right as it curves to the right, passing between the wall and the deep swallow-hole of Moor Pot and turning sharply downhill to the E.

6. Keep close to the wall (which now has a gill

on its other side) down rough pasture towards the Settle–Carlisle railway line seen ahead.

7. Bear slightly left on the final descent to a bridge over the railway at a cutting and reach the unfenced tarmac of Tommy Road just beyond it.

8. Turn right here and follow the road downhill to cross a cattle-grid. Follow the lane (now enclosed) downhill round a bend to cross Castle Bridge and find the ruins of Pendragon Castle just beyond, over the wall on the right. *See* page 160 for continuation of route into Kirkby Stephen.

Variation on the high-level route omitting Pendragon Castle

1. If through lack of time, inclination or even mistake, you do not follow the wall down the fellside towards Pendragon Castle as suggested above, continue along the track (the main one, keeping left (north) when it forks after leaving Little Fell) along the broad grassy ridge of Greenlaw Rigg.

2. With Tommy Road 200 yds in sight ahead, ensure you make the last part of the moorland descent so that an enclosed parcel of land, with a small barn in it, is on your immediate right.

3. Cross the tarmac and back onto open pasture and enter a walled green lane, seen ahead and with two barns on its left-hand side.

4. Follow this for ½ mile and at its end turn right over the Settle–Carlisle railway, then left on a track to a tarmac road.

5. Turn right here and immediately left on another track towards Low House, turning left again (N) in front of it. A concrete track now leads forward and in about ½ mile reaches a point where the main route joins from the right, near Mire Close Bridge.

6. From here you continue straight ahead, to pass Wharton Hall and complete the last short leg into Kirkby Stephen.

Day Four

Kirkby Stephen to Keld

➤ *Distance:* About 10½ miles/16.8km (the Green route – see text – is about 2 miles/3.2km longer)
➤ *Altitude gained:* About 1650 ft/503m
➤ *Terrain:* Initially on firm tarmac, then footpaths (occasionally ill-defined) over high peat moorland.
➤ *Refreshments:* Nil; stock up in Kirkby Stephen.

Excluding the option of walking all the way to Keld by road, the cross-country route, as far as the giant skyline cairns of the Nine Standards, coincides with the revised version of A. Wainwright's Coast to Coast Walk and is well signed on the ground. From the Nine Standards to the outskirts of Ravenseat, in order to allow the peaty ground to recover from the impact of booted feet, a management plan has been introduced which designates different routes for different times of the year, two being permissive paths, while the third uses public footpaths and some road. These have been designated the Green, Red and Blue routes. At the time of writing there is a map at Frank's Bridge showing these and they will be described in more detail shortly.

Kirkby Stephen to Nine Standards Rigg

1. Head E from the market square in the centre of Kirkby Stephen following a sign 'To Frank's Bridge and the River Eden'.
2. Once across the bridge turn right and follow a tarmac path to the E beside the River Eden, rising to a walled lane which is followed to a T-junction with a minor lane in Hartley village.

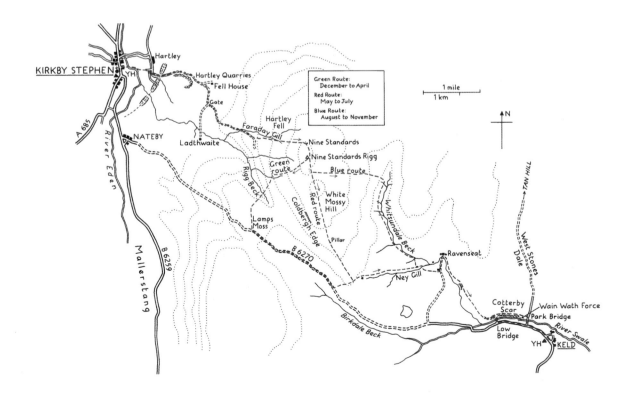

3. Turn right here and in 100 yds take a path on the left (yellow arrow) to cross Hartley Beck by a footbridge and join the road beyond, turning right and following it uphill.

4. The road continues climbing steeply, past the entrance to Hartley Quarry then, less steeply, continues past Fell House, on the left, to where the road forks, about 2 miles from Kirkby Stephen, having gained about 650 ft/198m of altitude this far.

5. The right-hand fork is signed for Lad-thwaite; take the left-hand one, signed 'Public Bridleway Rollinson Haggs'. There is a gate immediately ahead with a 'Coast to Coast' sign and 200 yds ahead a second gate and another sign: 'Coast to Coast Walk and Nine Standards. Due to severe ground damage the path has been re-routed. Please follow the waymarked permissive path.'

6. An obvious track now rises in a general direction just south of east, shortly with a wall on the right, then crossing a shallow beck (Faraday Gill). Continue with the beck on the left and rise to more finger-posts on a corner where the wall bends away to the right (SE). The sign pointing just south of east reads 'Permissive path Coast to Coast Walk and direct route to Nine Standards'.

7. This track climbs steadily, is marked by cairns and becomes a narrower path where it crosses peaty ground on small gritstone slabs. There is a last short rise to reach the giant cairns of the Nine Standards and to enjoy, if you are lucky, a tremendously far-ranging view.

8. From here a slightly uphill course just east of south (170 degrees grid) in 150 paces reaches a view indicator, then a further 300 paces or so on the same bearing leads to the OS column on Nine Standards Rigg.

Three Seasonal Routes from Nine Standards Rigg to Ney Gill

These three routes are designated and marked on the management map at Frank's Bridge as the Green route (December to April), the Red route (May to July) and the Blue route (August to November). The Red and Blue routes are virtually the same length while the Green route is 2 miles/3.2km longer. All routes converge at Ney Gill and from there lead forward to Ravenseat and thence by a common route (with a slight optional variation) into Keld.

The Green route to Ney Gill (*December–April*)

1. Head SW from the OS column on a faint path on the stony ground, which becomes more obvious once the peat is reached and is marked by occasional cairns. The path soon crosses the stream of Rollinson Gill, then crosses Rigg Beck (just outside the intake wall), shortly swinging S to traverse the limestone area of Lamps Moss and reach the B6270.

2. Turn left (SE) along the road for 1½ miles as far as a Land Rover track which turns off on the left.

3. Follow this track to the east for about ½ mile to a shooting-hut at the head of Ney Gill. (The Red route joins this track just before the shooting-hut.)

4. A reasonable path continues E down Ney Gill to a finger-post (at the point where the Blue route, the one down Whitsundale, also joins).

The Red route to Ney Gill (*May–July*)

1. From the OS column on Nine Standards Rigg, head just east of south (170 degrees grid) past a small collapsed stone shelter

and a cairn, close together, then slightly downhill to cross a wide and peaty grough with finger-posts on each side.

2. The Blue route diverges to the E here, following yellow-topped marker posts, but continue on the existing bearing just east of south (170 degrees grid) and slightly uphill to cross the top of White Mossy Hill.

3. In the same direction, now trending downhill, head for a prominent stone pillar about a mile away.

4. From the pillar continue SSE for a further ¾ mile to intersect with a Land Rover track (junction with the Green route).

5. Turn left here, shortly passing a shooting-hut, then continuing down Ney Gill to the finger-post.

The Blue route to Ney Gill via Whitsundale (*August–November*)

1. From the OS column head just east of south (170 degrees grid) as for the Red route past a small collapsed stone shelter and a cairn, then slightly downhill to cross a wide and peaty grough with finger-posts on each side.

2. From the post on the far side, where there is also a 'C to C' sign, the Red route continues straight ahead but the Blue route turns sharp left, leading almost due E and, following a line of yellow-topped marker-posters, declines gently to reach Whitsundale.

3. Another 'C to C' finger-post here indicates the path now shadowing Whitsundale Beck and further posts mark the way until a wire fence is crossed by a ladder-stile.

4. Just before reaching a transverse wall ahead there is a sharp change of direction to the right (S), marked by a finger-post, leading up a short slope to a stile, another finger-post and the ruins of a small barn which once had a curved roof of corrugated iron.

5. Down the short slope on the other side

is Ney Gill, where there is another finger-post.

Ney Gill to Keld

1. Head E, on a path between the beck in Ney Gill and the wall on the left, crossing to the other bank at a transverse wall (finger-post signed 'Keld 3').

2. Follow the wall up the bank on the other side, curving round to the left (E) again and keeping the wall on your left to reach the tarmac road into Ravenseat at a cattle-grid and gate.

3. Turn left towards the hamlet, trending right over two bridges and following yellow paint dots in front of the cottages to shadow the left (E) bank of Whitsundale Beck downstream.

4. The path, via several gates, passing several abandoned farm buildings and overlooking the gill below, passes by Oven Mouth, where part of the rocky bank has collapsed, then keeps to the right at a faintly-defined fork and to the right-hand side of a small enclosure.

5. Continue across open fellside to a finger-post ('Ravenseat ¾ Keld 1¾') and then to reach the partly derelict farm of Smithy Holme.

6. From here a broader track continues, slanting towards the River Swale, at Low Bridge, but before the last steeper descent watch for a yellow arrow sign on the left. This presents an option to follow the arrow and take a narrow path along the top of Cotterby Scar which, via two ladder-stiles, leads to the Tan Hill road on a bend. From here turn right and downhill to cross the Swale by Park Bridge, then turning left into Keld.

6a. Alternatively, continue down the broad track, cross the Swale by Low Bridge and turn left along the road and into Keld. This has more tarmac but better views of Cotterby Scar and Wain Wath Force.

Day Five

Keld to Reeth

➤ *Distance:* About 11¾ miles/18.8km on main route (about 12¾ miles/20.4km on high-level variation)

➤ *Altitude gained:* Negligible on main route (about 1000 ft/305m on high-level variation)

➤ *Terrain:* Good paths throughout the main route (and almost entirely so on the high-level route).

➤ *Refreshments:* In Muker (if you divert slightly) or in Gunnerside where there is a choice (both routes).

Today's main walk is a low-level route. The first part of the route descends the Swale gorge by the W bank, with an alternative using the E bank; both join at Ramps Holme Bridge. Thereafter, the main walk shadows the course of the Swale via Gunnerside and Healaugh to Reeth. There is, however, a high-level varia-tion from Gunnerside to Reeth to enable a walker to get some idea of the lead-mining history of Swaledale.

Keld to Ramps Holme Bridge via the west bank

1. Leave Keld by the walled lane signed for Muker, heading SE.

2. At the junction in about 300 yds, keep straight ahead (both ways signed Pennine Way).

3. In about 100 yds pass through a gate, then in a further 150 yds pass a finger-post signed 'FP Kisdon Upper Force' ignoring the footpath turning down to the left.

4. Keep on the main track for a further 200 yds or so, passing below a limestone scar on the right, to reach a large cairn (Pennine Way finger-post normally placed here) where the tracks diverge. The right-hand path is the Pennine Way; our route takes the left fork, climbing briefly to the top of a little rise (with a view down the Swale valley beyond) and then trending downhill towards the valley floor.

5. On this descent, to view the cascades of

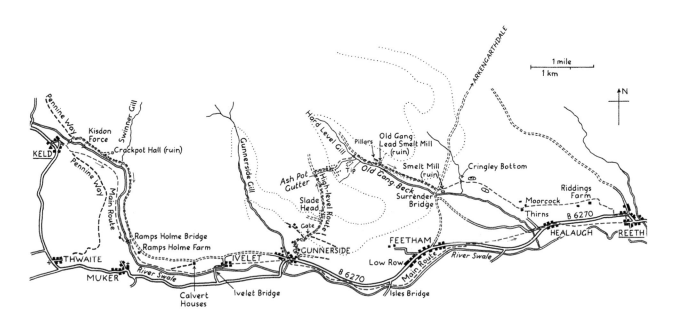

Kisdon Force, look for a stone gateway beside the track; from here a less-used path slants back down to the left to reach a good viewpoint on the limestone slabs beside the river. Return to the main track by reversing the way just used (a 15-minute diversion).

6. The now grassy path reaches the valley floor, going close to the river through a small alder wood and then, on the level, following yellow arrows to the left of a barn on the approach to Ramps Holme Bridge.

Alternative route to Ramps Holme Bridge via the east bank

1. Leave Keld by the walled lane signed for Muker, heading SE.
2. At the junction in about 300 yds turn left, downhill and down a sunken lane, bearing left at its end to a footbridge over the Swale.
3. Slant up the field beyond the footbridge (the path here is shared by both Pennine Way and Coast to Coast and there are finger-posts for both), passing by East Gill Force in a dell on the right. Reaching a good track at the top of the field, turn right (E) along it to pass directly above East Gill Force and through a gate just past it.
4. This track curves left round a bend, continues along the top of West Wood (with the Swale gorge below on the right), bends left again, passes a barn on the right and then, in about 150 yds or so, forks. Take the left-hand fork for a short distance to view the ruins of Crackpot Hall and the fine prospect down the Swale gorge.
5. Return to the main track, continuing downhill to the valley floor and so to a point opposite but slightly above Ramps Holme Bridge. Here slant down slightly to the right to join the path heading SE from the bridge itself

Ramps Holme Bridge to Gunnerside

1. Following the footpath SE from Ramps Holme Bridge, keep right at the fork in about 100 yds, signed 'Gunnerside via Ivelet'.
2. The path crosses meadows, almost touching the river, just S of the farm. It then cuts across the bend ahead, shadows the river again and then forks. Keep right here, following the river bank to Ivelet Bridge.
3. Follow the minor road left, still along the left bank of the Swale, turning uphill to the left into the hamlet of Ivelet.
4. Turn right in front of the phone box and shortly follow a signed path to a footbridge across a wooded beck. Slit-stiles now show the way across sloping meadows to Gunnerside village.

Gunnerside to near Feetham

1. Find the public toilets at the right-hand rear of the King's Head Inn and take the field path heading E from here across Gunnerside Bottoms, shadowing the road.
2. At the far side, at the top of a rise, join the road at a gate but immediately turn off the road again to the right and follow a path slanting back down to the riverside again.
3. Follow this path until forced onto the road again. In 200 yds leave the road at a gate on the right and take a grassy path leading back to the river (keeping left when the river encloses an island of pebble banks) and follow it to Isles Bridge.
4. Go left for 30 yds and then turn right (finger-post 'FP Reeth 3½') to follow the path along the broad top of a wall, then along a grassy embankment, by-passing both Low Row and Feetham and going through some woods until it turns sharply upslope to rejoin the B6270.

From near Feetham to Reeth

1. Turn right along the road for 300 yds, watch for the house named 'Robin Gate' on the left and take a footpath 'FP Healaugh' up a couple of steps immediately past the house.
2. A grassy path now traverses pastures above the main road, which is down on the right, reaching the Healaugh–Surrender Bridge road at the wooded gill of Barney Beck.
3. Turn right along tarmac here to rejoin the main road, turning left and uphill into and through Healaugh.
4. Reaching the green space at the far end of the village on the right, follow a signed way (finger-post 'Reeth') shadowing the road, via slit-stiles, towards Reeth. On the approach, keep left of a wall so that you are funnelled into a walled lane; at its end footpath signs direct you into Reeth. Walkers not staying overnight close to the centre of the village may find this a good opportunity to stock up with supplies.

High-level variation: Gunnerside to Reeth via Surrender Bridge

Note: This variation is about 1 mile/1.6km further than the main low-level route and has an extra altitude gain of about 1000 ft/305m.

A fairly steep climb out of Gunnerside leads to an easy crossing of the high moor and gradual descent via Hard Level Gill and Old Gang Beck to Surrender Bridge. Thereafter, following the Coast to Coast path, a mid-height traverse on good paths above Healaugh leads to a descent to Reeth.

Gunnerside to Surrender Bridge

1. Walk out of Gunnerside going E towards Reeth along B6270 and in about 200 yds turn left uphill up a tarmac drive signed as a cul de sac.
2. This climbs sharply and in about 50 yds the tarmac strip (which is an infallible guide onto the moor above) makes a sharp left-hand bend. Follow this round (ignoring the unmade walled track continuing E) as it is both footpath and unfenced service road for a number of houses and converted barns higher up. This tarmac strip continues to rise to the N in steep zigzags, but when the angle eases, it appears to be heading for buildings at Potting. However, a ravine intervenes, forcing the strip to turn right (E) to skirt its edge, on the left.
3. The tarmac strip shortly comes to an end at a gate through an intake wall, just above a half-derelict barn and nearby finger-post for a footpath for Low Row, pointing SE. (This is at grid ref 956987, S of spot height 405m).
4. The objective now is the junction of paths at the grouse butts on Slade Head. Take a grassy track to the right, beyond the gate, heading NE, keeping left in 100 yds and climbing NE onto open moor.
5. The track forks at the 490m contour (about 1600 ft/488m) and you keep right (N) shortly to pass a line of stone grouse butts on Slade Head. To the right (NE) long heather slopes head to Hard Level Gill but follow the obvious four-wheel-drive track northwards, contouring to cross the stream of Ash Pot Gutter at a ford.
6. Immediately beyond it, turn right (E) and

follow a good gravel track downhill, past more grouse butts, to its end, continuing beyond to pass a large disused spoil-tip and reach a gated causeway across Hard Level Gill.

7. Follow the main track down the gill on its far side, shortly passing the stone pillars and then the ruins of Old Gang Lead Smelt Mill (the Coast to Coast path has now been joined), to reach Surrender Bridge.

Surrender Bridge to Reeth

1. Cross the unfenced tarmac road at a 'Footpath' finger-post, keeping left when it forks and passing above the ruins of the Surrender Bridge Smelt Mill.

2. A reasonable path leads forward to the ENE, with occasional boggy bits, and soon crosses the ravine of Cringley Bottom.

3. From a gated slit-stile on its far bank, a pleasant grass track leads E with a wall alongside for the first 500 yds. When the wall ends, continue forwards but veering right (SE) passing an enclosure with an isolated barn on the left (Cleasby). In 500 yds after the wall ends keep to the higher of two paths to pass to the left (N) of a two-field isolated enclosure.

4. The path now becomes more of a cart track, funnelling downhill between walls, by-passing a cottage in an enclosure on the left and reaching the farm at Thirns.

5. Turn left here, uphill, on a concreted slope, to pass directly in front of the isolated cottage named 'Moorcock'. From here a good track climbs slightly, passing through a zone of old spoil-tips then contours just above the intake wall.

6. When this track, after the point where there is a sharp right turn into the property at Riddings, becomes little more than a green trod sloping down towards Riddings Farm, slant leftwards (still going E) at a higher level on a well-used path to a cairn. Just beyond, rounding a wall corner is the gated and walled Skelgate Lane.

7. Follow this, sunken in parts and fairly overgrown with vegetation, to the B6270 road, where a left turn leads directly into Reeth. Walkers who are not staying overnight close to the centre of Reeth may find this a good opportunity to stock up on any necessary supplies for the final day's walk to Richmond.

Looking east over Cringley Bottom towards Reeth

Day Six

Reeth to Richmond

➤ *Distance:* About 10½ miles/16.8km
➤ *Altitude gained:* About 750 ft/229m
➤ *Terrain:* Mostly on good paths and tracks, but occasionally very faint across some pastures where care is needed.
➤ *Refreshments:* Stock up in Reeth as there are no other opportunities until Richmond.

After about a mile on the Swale's north bank, the route rises to the NE and crosses two low ridges via Marrick and Marske. It then traverses a wide shelf just below the limestone scars on the north bank of the Swale before entering Richmond. 'Coast to Coast' signs and yellow-arrow waymarks help navigation.

Reeth to Marrick

1. From Reeth head E on the main road to cross Arkle Beck at Reeth Bridge, then in 200 yds take a signed footpath on the right across level pastures to reach the Swale at Grinton Bridge. Cross the bridge to view Grinton church, the finest in Swaledale, but then return to the N bank.

1a. (From Grinton Lodge Youth Hostel simply walk back downhill to the N side of Grinton Bridge.)

2. A signed footpath now shadows the N bank of the Swale, shortly rising slightly to join the metalled track leading SE to Marrick Abbey Farm and the ruins of Marrick Priory.

3. Just beyond the buildings take a path slanting left to enter Steps Wood, rising over ancient stone flags with a wall on the right. After leaving the wood and with the wall still beside you, the now grassy path reaches a gate beside a barn, with a small gated enclosure on its other side. A double finger-

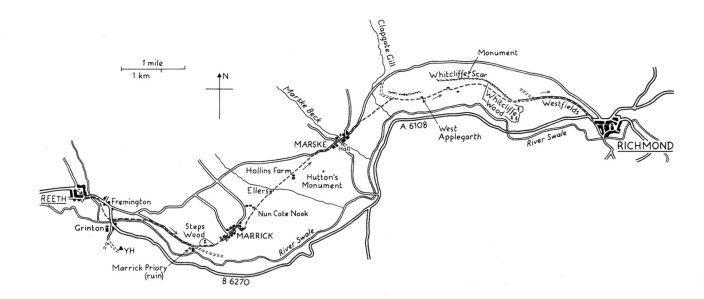

post here may raise doubts, but keep to the left, the continuation of the path you are already on. It leads into Marrick at a gate, with a converted Wesleyan Chapel (1878) on the left.

Marrick to Marske Bridge

1. Follow the metalled road through the village, bearing to the left and then right at a T-junction (public phone box almost opposite). Pass the Village Institute and at the fork ahead bear right (SE, C-to-C finger-post) passing 'The Old School House' and Park Lodge (next to it) where the tarmac ends.

2. A 'Coast to Coast' finger-post points N from the corner of this last house into a lane which in 50 yds turns rightwards into a field, where it peters out. Instead of turning into the field, continue ahead (NNE) to a slit-stile directly ahead and then follow yellow arrows through more stiles close together, still NNE and close to some old railway goods wagons used as animal shelters, and a large modern barn.

3. Moving away from the farm, this path crosses more fields, rising gently to higher land and trending slightly further east, to give a greatly expanded view of surrounding terrain and with Hutton's Monument visible on high ground to the ENE, just to the right of the line of march.

4. The path now descends a convex slope towards the valley of Ellers Beck, crossing the farm track to Nun Cote Nook, then signposts point to the NE down two large fields to reach the isolated, converted house of Ellers, on the bank of the beck of the same name.

5. Crossing the footbridge behind the house, a path rises NE to a gate in a field corner, then to the top left of a strand of trees sheltering Hollins Farm.

6. The OS map shows the right-of-way path rising half-right (NE) across the track and up the sloping pasture ahead. A low wire fence traverses this, across the line of march, but if you look to the right along the track you may spot a gate that can be used to avoid having to step over the wire. Continue slanting rightwards up the field beyond to its right-hand side, turning upslope beside the wall to a stile. Just beyond is a finger-post and gate through the wall on the right.

7. Continue NE over a slight rise, then slant NE down the field beyond, joining the Reeth–Marske road opposite a cottage at Hardstiles Top.

8. Turn right onto the road which leads steeply downhill to Marske Bridge, in a wooded hollow.

Marske Bridge to Whitcliffe Wood

1. Walk up the road (road sign 'Whashton and Ravensworth') to Marske village. Turn right at the T-junction and continue uphill; as the houses are left behind and you begin to go slightly downhill, find a slit-stile on the right, on the second bend after leaving the T-junction.

2. From here the path leads via five stiles across a wide dip channelling the Clapgate Beck, crossed by a footbridge, towards the wooded limestone flanks of Applegarth Scar facing you.

3. From the footbridge an obvious path rises past a telegraph pole to a white-washed cairn beside a level cart-track just below Applegarth Scar.

4. The track leads to West Applegarth Farm, passes in front of the buildings and then apparently peters out but, 100 yds ahead, there is a stone barn, with a gate beside it.

5. Turn right through the gate and then sharp left to pass in front of the barn and resume

the easterly direction, traversing the pastures sloping down to the wooded Swale valley below on the right. Stiles lead to where you cross a tarmac track (to Low Applegarth).

6. Either turn left and follow the track as it curves round to the right, or continue across another pasture to rejoin the same track immediately past the renovated barn at High Applegarth, but take the path signed off to the left just before reaching it.

7. This path soon becomes a delightful grass way contouring below Whitcliffe Scar and leading into Whitcliffe Wood at a gate.

Whitcliffe Wood to Richmond

1. Emerging from the wood, the track passes High Leases (farm) on the right and soon becomes a tarmac lane, with a distant view of Richmond ahead.

2. This lane undulates for a way and then begins a long descent down the pleasant suburban road of Westfields and into Richmond.

3. The most interesting entry into this ancient and very attractive town is by crossing Reeth Road (at the end of Westfields) into Cravengate, taking first left into Newbiggin and then second right down Finkle Street into the Market Square.

Grinton church, and the bridge over the River Swale

The Short Cut

Hawes to Thwaite & Muker over Great Shunner Fell

➤ *Distance:* About 10½ miles/16.8km (to Muker)
➤ *Altitude gained:* About 1600 ft/488m
➤ *Terrain:* Over high gritstone moorland, but most of the boggier stretches are now traversed by stone slabs so it is comparatively easy walking.
➤ *Refreshments:* At Hardraw, Thwaite and in Muker.

It must be emphasised that this short cut is emphatically not a low-level easy option as it is exposed to bad weather like all the high Pennine fells. It is strongly recommended that accommodation in Swaledale should be pre-booked by phone from Hawes. The most extensive accommodation guide appears to be the *Coast to Coast Guide* (*see* Introduction) and

there is a choice of B&Bs between Thwaite and Gunnerside, although the only Youth Hostel is at Keld, 3 miles away, uphill and in the wrong direction. It is a little over 13 miles from Hawes to Gunnerside, and obviously less if accommodation is found before reaching Gunnerside. The diagram on the following page should prove helpful.

Hawes to Hardraw

This is a reversal of the last part of yesterday's walk (Day 2).

1. From the car park at the National Park Centre at the east end of Hawes (grid ref 876898) take the road going north-east towards Sedbusk and Hardraw.
2. In about 200 yds take a stone-flagged path on the left, signed Pennine Way, which cuts off a corner.
3. Rejoin the road, following it to cross the River Ure at Haylands Bridge, then take the second footpath on the left, up a few stone steps and also signed 'Pennine Way'. A good path leads across pastures, becoming a stone-flagged causeway which leads to the road in

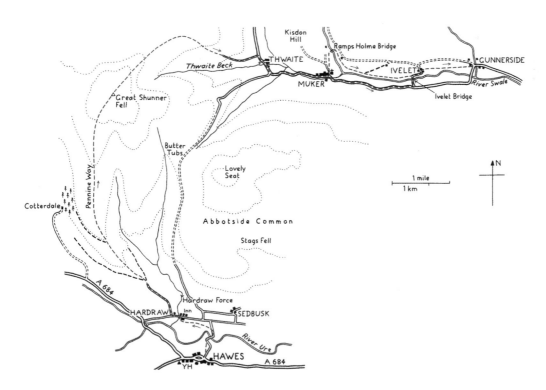

Hardraw, directly opposite the Green Dragon pub. If you did not do so yesterday, this is a good opportunity to visit the superb Hardraw Falls, reached through the pub premises.

Hardraw to Great Shunner Fell

1. Leaving the Green Dragon, turn right (W) past the church, over the bridge and past Harris House. Take the first turn after this, a walled lane, with a finger-post pointing NW, signed 'FP Thwaite 8 (PW)'.
2. Follow the lane to the fell gate at its end.
3. Almost immediately the track ahead forks; take the left-hand fork (Pennine Way finger-post).
4. In 200 yds, another finger-post marks where a grassy trod veers left towards Cotterdale, but stay on the right fork, now rising over open moor and along the crest of a broad ridge, close to a wall on the left, then rising to a gate and quite large sheepfold.
5. In 50 yds the track forks again, the left-hand one signed 'BW Cotterdale 3km', but stay on the right fork marked by a Pennine Way finger-post pointing NNW and confirmed by cairns ahead. There are no further side tracks or paths to confuse the issue: it is now a straightforward plod.
6. Stay on the path, passing a half-collapsed sheepfold then crossing some boggy ground by duckboards but increasingly using stone flags forming sections of causeway. A stone column or beacon is passed close to the track which follows the curve of the broad ridge ahead and leads to the hollowed-out heap of stones on top of Great Shunner Fell.

Great Shunner Fell to Thwaite and Muker

1. The path leads off to the NE, in a wide curve along the high land to the north of feeder streams flowing into Thwaite Beck, passing another beacon en route.
2. After about 1½ miles a more noticeable descent leads to a gate at the end of a walled lane. In 1 mile this joins the B6270 road north of Thwaite.
3. Turn right, downhill, into Thwaite.
4. Walk E along the road to Muker about 1 mile further on.

Dependent on accommodation plans and time in hand, the route of the main walk, Day Five from Keld to Reeth, will be picked up from Muker. If time is pressing, stay on the road east of Muker to the turn off for Ivelet Bridge, at Oxnop, and the road on the north side of the bridge leads into Ivelet. From here pick up the last part of the walk into Gunnerside, as described on page 167.

If time is not pressing, it is scenically well worth heading north out of Muker, to Ramps Holme Bridge, to pick up the very attractive footpath on the north bank of the River Swale. Entering Muker from Thwaite, continue to the east end of the village, turning left in front of the Literary Institute. Follow the metalled road to where it veers left in front of the post office, but then keep right to find a signpost for Gunnerside and Keld. A series of stiles now lead across meadowland to the river bank and Ramps Holme Bridge. The rest of the way is described in detail in Day Five's 'Ramps Holme Bridge to Gunnerside', *see* page 167.

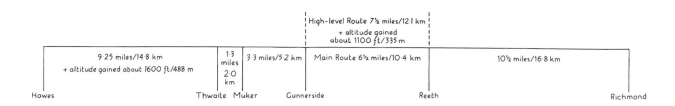

A Record of the Journey

Below Penhill, looking west

DAY/STAGE	COMMENTS

Day One: *Leyburn to Aysgarth*

Main route
abt 8 miles/12.8km
via Wensley
Lords Bridge
Redmire Force

High-level route via Penhill
abt 12½ miles/20km
via Middleham
Penhill Farm
High Lane

Day Two: *Aysgarth to Hawes*

abt 12½ miles/20km
via Carperby
Askrigg
Skell Gill
Sedbusk
Hardraw

Day Three: *Hawes to Kirkby Stephen*

Main route
abt 15½ miles/24.8km
via Cotter End
Hell Gill Bridge
The Thrang
Shoregill

(Day Three *contd*)
Pendragon Castle
   via Outhgill and B6259
   via field path
Lammerside Castle

High-level route – Hell Gill Bridge to
   Pendragon Castle via Wild Boar Fell
adding abt 4 miles / 6.4km in total
via Aisgill Moor Cottages
Wild Boar Fell
Tommy Road

Day Four: *Kirkby Stephen to Keld*

abt 10 ½ miles / 16.8km
   (or 12 ½ miles / 19km on Green route)
via Nine Standards Rigg
Ney Gill
   via Green route
   via Red route
   via Blue route

Day Five: *Keld to Reeth*

Main route
abt 11 ¾ miles / 18.8km
via Ramps Holme Bridge
   via the west bank
   via the east bank
Gunnerside
Feetham

High-level route – Gunnerside to Reeth via Surrender Bridge
adding abt 1 mile/1.6km in total
via Surrender Bridge

Day Six: *Reeth to Richmond*

abt 10½ miles/16.8km
via Marrick
Marske Bridge
Whitcliffe Wood

The Short Cut: *Hawes to Thwaite & Muker over Great Shunner Fell*

abt 11½ miles/16.8km (to Muker)
via Hardraw
Great Shunner Fell

The author welcomes *sensible* comments from readers/walkers after this walk has been completed; any adjustments could then be inserted in to the next printing. Please write to Bob Allen c/o Michael Joseph Limited, 27 Wrights Lane, London W8 5TZ, marking your envelope A DALES WALK; please enclose a stamped addressed envelope if a reply is needed.